FIRST, DO NO UNJUST HARM

Recognizing and Confronting Evil

John S. Pletz

University Press of America,® Inc.
Lanham · Boulder · New York · Toronto · Oxford

Copyright © 2003 by
University Press of America,® Inc.
4501 Forbes Boulevard
Suite 200
Lanham, Maryland 20706
UPA Acquisitions Department (301) 459-3366

PO Box 317
Oxford
OX2 9RU, UK

ISBN 0-7618-2587-8 (paperback : alk. ppr.)

CONTENTS

PART I
RECOGNIZING EVIL AND
OTHER FORMS OF IMMORALITY

PART II:
CONFRONTING EVIL AND OTHER
FORMS OF IMMORALITY

ACKNOWLEDGMENTS

Thanks are owed to many for their assistance to me in the development of this book.

Access to Ellis Library at the University of Missouri-Columbia under its open stack policy allowed me to do a considerable amount of research in a limited amount of time, and for that I am grateful to the Library and to the University Curators.

I want to extend belated appreciation to Professors Lawrence C. Becker of The College of William and Mary and Robert Van Wyk of The University of Pittsburgh at Johnstown for their comments and encouragement on my first book, *Being Ethical*. I would also like to thank Dr. Irma Korte for her helpful support and Deborah S. Peterson for her editorial assistance.

Finally, my thanks to my wife, Karen, and to my daughters, Brittany and Casey, for the tolerance and forbearance they have shown as I have devoted time and efforts to these pursuits.

INTRODUCTION

If you share in the fundamental notion that people either are, or should be, basically good, then it is distressing when you first realize that the full spectrum of evils which we can collectively imagine not only have been perpetrated, but also that they are often still being done. Whether evils are described in general terms or by means of graphic examples, every conceivable sort of evil has been committed. Such actions now vary only with respect to their details and embellishments. The simple fact is that evil is a regular and frequent occurrence in and around all of our lives.

Unfortunately, this fact does not seem to be very effectively offset by the recognition that the contraries are true as well: Whatever types and examples of good that we can imagine have also been done and often continue to be done, and goodness is also a regular and frequent occurrence in our lives. This insight may be salvific for specific persons or particular groups at certain points of time and in the context of certain events; but the fact that we also do good does not seem to redeem us in the face of all of the evil that we do. As a species, our overall sense of morality still appears to be in question, in spite of the fact that we have made certain clear ethical advances over the centuries.

However, once we recognize the existence of evil and its extent, then, if we also share in the fundamental impulse of hope and have some degree of commitment to the virtue of benevolence, we look for ways to do something about it. But before we can effectively do anything at all about evil, we must first be able to accurately discern when it is present. It does no good—and indeed, it does harm—to oppose and punish the wrong things (that is, actions which are either right or not clearly wrong). In order to direct our limited energies and efforts against genuine wrongs, we need to know what evil is, and we need to avoid confusing it with things which are good or morally neutral.

If we do go astray in making such judgments, we can cause irremediable harm. A clear example of this would be the execution of an innocent man wrongly convicted of murder. Because we can—and often do—intentionally cause a lot of harm to suspected evildoers, and because we may also unintentionally cause considerable harm to innocent people in the process, identifying evil accurately is a matter of moral duty.

We also need to be able to identify different types and degrees of evil reliably, and especially to distinguish between major and minor evils. This makes it possible to exercise appropriate restraint in responding to a situation in which we have determined that some evil is present. Most of us can and do hate some of evil's most odious manifestations with a burning and vengeful passion. However, even when we are sure that it really is evil that we are opposing, we need to understand both its context and its degree as we formulate a response to it; because overreaction can propagate new evils in and of themselves. Such an overreaction can, indeed, turn what we might have begun as an ethical enterprise (the opposition of evil) into an unethical one (the commission of evil in the name of good). If we punish "minor" evils, or those which occur in cases in which mitigating factors are present, in the same way as we punish "major" evils, then our actions may fail their own ethical review. Justice requires us to treat others fairly, and we do not succeed at this when we are excessive in meting out punishments.

While the identification of evil is tremendously important, it is not always easy. We may not like to acknowledge this, because we usually believe that we know the most egregious evils whenever we see them. We hardly feel any need for definitions or analysis when, for example, a mass murderer is apprehended. But the nature of other evil, in particular some of the "lesser" degrees of immorality, is not always so clear to us. If you stop to reflect about the specific things that others have recently told you were "bad," you will probably recognize that you may have rejected some of those designations, or at least had difficulty in accepting some of them: Maybe all of them were "bad," maybe not; maybe they were all "evil," but maybe not. Still greater difficulties sometimes become apparent when disparate groups of people try to differentiate degrees of wrongfulness in efforts to separate "lesser evils" from "greater evils."

This lack of accord shows that, at least at times, some of us experience serious problems in identifying evil. We all hear people who say (and think) that they are actively (and righteously) opposing evil when their actions appear to contradict this claim. Even more disturbing is the fact that we are often confronted by credible and responsible individuals and groups that stand in opposition to each other on the question of the morality of certain actions. One person says that doing "X" is an evil act, and the other contradicts this and says that doing "X" is good. If you accept the basic rules of logic (in this case, the law of non-contradiction), then both of these people cannot be correct. So how can we determine which, if either of them, is?

This is by no means merely an academic exercise. We need to be able to identify evil and other forms of immorality so that we may deal more effectively with them. This knowledge is essential to our efforts. Given the present state of moral affairs in our world (and unfortunately, many people could have voiced the same concern at almost any point in recorded history), few could cogently argue that we do not need to better deal with the problems of evil. And, if we really want to, we *can* often do so, even though, as in many of our other endeavors, this may frequently require work. In light of the fact that we have this capability, however, we have a continuing moral obligation to try to sharpen our powers of judgment in this area.

The objectives of this book are to suggest some specific approaches to the identification and analysis of evil and other forms of immorality, and then to propose some ways in which we may personally perform our ethical duty of confronting it. While this is but one of our moral duties, it is among the most important.

PART I

✿

RECOGNIZING EVIL AND OTHER FORMS OF IMMORALITY

1

A Brief Survey of Thoughts
About the Nature of Evil

P eople have been thinking about good and evil at least several millennia, as shown by the many early recorded thoughts on these concepts. Nevertheless, it is interesting to note how relatively little writing in the area of ethics focuses on evil, as compared to that which focuses on good. One reason for this may be that when we consider the broad questions of morality, we more often think about good than we do about evil because we have been motivated either by a desire to do good (or at least to improve in our efforts at doing good), or by a need to understand why other people think they know what good is and why it seems to motivate them so. Certainly the question, "How can we know what is good so that we can do what is good?" has more resonance and has engaged more people than its converse. Fortunately, the question "How can we know what is bad so that we can do what is bad?" seems generally to interest fewer of us (with the exception of two-year-olds and others in rebellious stages of their lives). In other words, few people seek to pursue evil because it is evil—at least for very long. Rather, most of those who do evil are primarily engaged in the pursuit of other personal benefits and simply disregard the consequences of their actions for others; in any given moment when they are acting, they are not particularly concerned about ethical issues underlying their choices or about the nature of their actions.

Even when we are trying to focus on the good and the ethical, however, we cannot ignore the question of evil. Its analysis is necessary to a comprehensive understanding of ethics because good and evil are endpoints of the same moral continuum—with its extremes of the very good and the very bad. Furthermore, one of our major ethical duties is to avoid and oppose evil. If we do not understand the moments when evil dominates as well as those in which it is overcome, we will not be able to avoid and oppose it as effectively as we otherwise might.

Another reason why less has been written on immorality than on morality is that, over the centuries, our leaders have wanted to act with great certainty with respect to problems created by evil and its particular manifestations. There are significant practical benefits in being able to condemn an action in the complete assurance that it is wrong, because a key element in fighting evil is in the strength of our motivation. We are more strongly impelled to act when we are not in doubt about an action in any way. Such an unambiguous stance has been advantageous to our dominant institutions, including our governments, in fostering acceptance of, rather than debate about, their pronouncements on evil (and thus also on their enemies). Analyzing evil may raise some doubts about particular events or actions that have been labeled "evil," and the public expression of those doubts could lead to a weakening of support for some of the ideological commitments inherent in the policies of our dominant institutions. For this reason, those in control of these institutions have tended neither to appreciate nor to encourage speculation about the identity and nature of immorality; they know what they want us to oppose.

A third reason why less has been written about the nature of evil, at least in Western literature, is that the central issue in many discussions on the subject has been whether the existence of evil and the existence of God are or should be mutually exclusive. This is commonly referred to as "the problem of evil."[1] Conventionally

---

1. See, for example, the only entry under "evil" in *The Encyclopedia of Philosophy,* which is "The Problem of Evil," Paul Edwards, ed.,

stated, given that God is good and that God created the world, and given that the world has a lot of evil in it, logic suggests that one or more of the following conclusions should follow: (a) God created evil; (b) God somehow is not powerful enough to prevent the existence of evil or to stop all the evil in this world; or (c) God does not love us the way we would expect to be loved by a loving God, because if He did, He would not allow so many bad things to happen to us. Most of the literature on "the problem of evil" presents various arguments against these conclusions, but the writers rarely try to further identify or analyze evil itself. Rather, a comprehension of the nature of evil is assumed by them, and they have moved on to a subsequent and, in their view, more interesting and significant topic.[2]

While "the problem of evil" is an important subject, it is not a primary subject of this book. Rather, I am more interested in the prior question, namely, that of trying to understand what evil and immorality are.

Although more ethical literature focuses on the nature of good than on that of evil, literary works as a whole do not ignore or underplay evil. Indeed, the converse is true. In much of our literature (particularly fiction), evil gets a tremendous amount of ink (and celluloid). Most people are fascinated—and sometimes trans-fixed—by stories about evil and the suffering it causes, just as many of us are drawn to stare at automobile accidents that we pass on highways. And many stories, even if they are not directly with evil (exceptions including Fyodor Dostoyevsky's *Crime and Punishment* or Herman Melville's *Moby Dick*), at least have important plot elements that are concerned with it or with potential evil. Such storytelling can be not only highly entertaining but also informative and instructive; but while such stories may present great object lessons in a manner that has substantial impact, they do not directly analyze evil, nor do they usually advise us how we can identify it in other settings or circumstances.

Macmillan Publishing Co., (New York, 1967), vol. 3, p. 136.
2. This is not to suggest that those who have concerned themselves with the problem of evil have not comprehended it, but rather only that discussions about it are not common in their works.

A full survey of the history of thought on the subject of evil and other forms of immorality is far beyond the scope of this book.[3] A brief survey is, however, necessary in order to place this endeavor in context and to provide a foundation and perspective for its development. To further narrow its scope, the primary focus of the first several chapters will be on evil, rather than the broader question of immorality—this despite the fact that the subject of this book is the identification of and confrontation with not only evil, but also other types of immorality. If we accept the proposition that the word "evil" applies to the worst kind of immorality—that, in fact, it is always to be found at the bottom of the moral continuum—then evil should be the clearest example of immorality and the easiest of its aspects to comprehend and to define. Methodologically, it would seem to be reasonable to work first on the clearest examples of the object of our study. This should facilitate understanding and thus avoid diversions. When we have done a thorough job in analyzing these examples, we can proceed more easily to areas which are less clear (in this case, up the moral continuum through immorality to the beginning of either morality or amorality[4]).

Surveys such as this appropriately start with a discussion of the common consensus we have arrived at for basic definitions of terms. I will therefore begin with the definition of the English word "evil" as provided in our dictionaries, then progress to some reflections on the meaning of the word and its uses in both religious and philosophical sources, and finally move on to some of its applications in the mass media and popular culture.

The definitions of the word "evil," taken from three major English language dictionaries, are set out in the margins below for reference.[5] While the word can be used either as a noun or as an

---

3. For a contemporary comprehensive survey, see Susan Neiman's *Evil in Modern Thought*, Princeton University Press (2002).
4. Which in turn depends upon whether it is appropriate to describe a middle zone in the morality continuum between the good and the bad—another issue beyond the scope of this book.
5. *Webster's Third New International Dictionary of the English Language Unabridged*, Philip Babcock Gove, ed., G. & C. Merriam Co. (Springfield, MA, 1976), p. 789: *adj*...1a: not good morally:

marked by bad moral qualities: violating the rules of morality: WICKED, SINFUL...b: arising from actual or imputed bad character or conduct...2a: *archaic*: unsound or inferior in quality: WORTHLESS, POOR...b: causing discomfort or repulsion: UNCOMFORTABLE, OFFENSIVE, PAINFUL, FOUL...c: ANGRY, DISAGREEABLE, UNPLEASANT, WRATHFUL, MALIGNANT...3a: causing or tending to cause harm: BANEFUL, HARMFUL, PERNICIOUS...b: portending harm or misfortune...c: WRETCHED, MISERABLE, UNFORTUNATE...d: marked or signalized by misfortune or calamity: UNLUCKY, INAUSPICIOUS. *n*...1a: the fact of suffering and wickedness: the totality of undesirable, harmful, wicked acts, experiences, and things....b: a cosmic force producing evil actions or states...c(1) WICKEDNESS, SIN...(2): the wicked or undesirable element or portion of anything...d(1): evil actions or deeds—used chiefly with *do*...(2): slanderous or malicious speech...(3): an evil person: one that embodies or personifies wickedness...2a: something that is injurious to moral or physical happiness or welfare: MISFORTUNE, CALAMITY, DISASTER... *esp*: something...that has harmful effects...b: a harmful consequence: ill effect...3: MALADY, DISEASE....

The New Shorter Oxford English Dictionary on Historical Principles, Lesley Brown, ed., Clarendon Press (Oxford, 1993), p. 867. n. 1 Wickedness, moral depravity, sin; whatever is censurable, painful, malicious, or disastrous; the evil part or element of anything. 2 A wrongdoing, a crime, a sin... 3 *the evil, (collect. pl.)* people. 4 A disaster, a misfortune... 5 a disease, a sickness... b Hist. *the (king's) evil*, scrofula... 6 Any particular thing that is physically or morally harmful. a 1 Morally depraved, bad, wicked. 2 Causing pain or trouble; unpleasant, offensive, disagreeable... 3 Unsound, unwholesome; poor, unsatisfactory; defective... 4 Harmful, prejudicial; malicious; boding ill... 5 a Of conditions, fortune, etc.: unfortunate, miserable... b of a period of time: characterized by misfortune; unlucky, disastrous....

Random House Unabridged Dictionary, Second Edition, Stuart Berg Flexner, ed., Random House (New York, 1993), p. 672. adj. 1. morally wrong or bad; immoral; wicked... 2. harmful, injurious;... 3. characterized or accompanied by misfortune or suffering; unfortunate; disastrous... 4. due to actual or imputed bad conduct or adjective without substantial deviation in sense, when we eliminate the archaic meanings, we find two basic themes in these definitions. One of those focuses on harm and suffering ("harmful," "injurious," "misfortune," "suffering," "disastrous," "undesirable," "painful," "troubling," "miserable"), and the other centers around wickedness and immorality ("morally wrong," "immoral," "wicked," "bad conduct, character or disposition," "sinful," "malicious," "corrupt," "depraved," "unrighteous," "censurable"). Of the latter sense, the dictionaries say that evil is "not good morally" or "morally bad."

The clusters of meanings in the first group (which focus on harm and suffering) are not concerned with causes or blame. On this understanding of the term, when there is suffering, there is evil. ("The school fell upon evil days"; "Much evil shall happen to you"; "To wish one evil.") This is sometimes referred to as the broad definition of evil. Using it we would claim that evil was present in conditions or incidents that cause suffering (e.g., poverty, injury, disease and other such ills), regardless of the identity or nature of their causes.

The clusters of meanings in the second group (which focus on wickedness and immorality) require consideration of causation and involve the issue of moral blame. On this meaning of the term (the narrow definition), evil is equivalent to the morally bad. ("An evil piece of work," "evil laws," "an evil disposition," "evil men.")

It could be argued that even the broad definition of evil would imply certain things about causation and blame if our world view includes the acknowledgment of active malevolent spirits. We might then attribute all pain and suffering—or evil broadly defined—to a malicious animus (e.g., Satan, Shiva, demons, or some other negative spirits). However, it appears that the broad definition has

---

character... 5. marked by anger, irritability, irascibility, etc.... 6. the evil one, the devil; Satan... n. 7. that which is evil; evil quality, intention, or conduct... 8. the force in nature that governs and gives rise to wickedness and sin... 9. the wicked or immoral part of someone or something... 10. harm; mischief; misfortune... 11. anything causing injury or harm... 12. a harmful aspect, effect, or consequence... 13. a disease, as king's evil... 14. in an evil manner; badly; ill....

primarily been used to mean harm or suffering by itself and not to imply or require the consideration of its causes. "Evil" in the broad sense is a label we use to identify something as being or bringing horrible harm and suffering in and of itself, and it seems to carry with it little if anything by way of attribution or causation.

The word "evil" as it is currently used is rarely employed in the broad sense, but rather is almost always used in the narrow moral sense. If someone is struck by lightening, we call it "horrible" and "awful" and "terrible," but we usually do not call it "evil" (absent intervening human causes that may have put that person in harm's way). That is, we no longer tend to call every accidental or unpreventable incident that brings undeserved harm "evil." Furthermore, if we wanted to use the word "evil" very often in the broad sense, then, in order to differentiate between its first and second meanings, we would have to feel comfortable adding qualifying phrases for the latter like "immoral evil," "culpable evil," and "evil with evil intent"; but such phrases sound both strange and redundant. Hence, the broad use of the term has become more or less outdated (with the exception of certain traditional employments of it, such as in discussions about "the problem of evil" or in the phrase "deliver us from evil" in the Lord's Prayer, which is usually understood in the broad sense— even though that phrase may have begun as "deliver us from the evil one,"[6] and even though the intention behind it may be to ask that we be delivered from doing evil ourselves). We now customarily use other words to describe the natural disasters and terrible tragedies that are not attributable to an identifiable causal agent. This is, at least in part, the result of advances in scientific understanding which have better identified the causes of many of the pains and harms that occur in our lives.

Consequently, we now essentially use the word "evil" not for *all* harm, but rather for harm that emanates from immorality. That is,

---

6. See, e.g., *International Standard Bible Encyclopedia*, Geoffrey W. Bromiley, ed., William B. Eerdmans Pub. Co. (Grand Rapids, Mich., 1982), pp.207-208. When we are praying for general protection, we probably want protection not only from harm caused as a part of an evil activity by someone else but also from all other kinds of harms, as well.

when we employ the word "evil," we are usually making a moral judgment about the cause of that harm. The narrow definition of "evil" can thus be characterized as "harm-plus": in other words, the narrow definition is the old broad definition plus the element of immorality. Harm by itself was the broad view; harm with culpability is the narrow, and now more generally used, definition of "evil."

While lexicographers would maintain that the broad usage retains some current validity, the cluster of definitions dealing with the lower end of the morality/immorality continuum is, as noted earlier, the subject of this book. Therefore, from this point forward, when I use the word "evil," it is meant in the second, morality-based sense.

The next step in this survey will be a review of some of our primary sources of traditional wisdom on this question. The ancient texts that grapple with good and evil have, in large part, provided the foundations for our major religions. Because every culture and age must wrestle with these issues, a tremendous repository of wisdom has been developed on the subject.

The English word "evil" appears 573 times in the Revised Standard Version of the Bible—464 times in the Old Testament, 43 times in the Gospels, and 66 times in the rest of the New Testament.[7] It first appears in Genesis 2:9:

> Out of the ground the Lord God made to grow every tree that is pleasant to the sight and good for food, the tree of life also in the midst of the garden, and the tree of the knowledge of good and evil.

It last appears in Revelations 22:11:

> Let the evildoer still do evil, and the filthy still be filthy, and the righteous still do right, and the holy still be holy.

---

7. *Nelson's Complete Concordance of the Revised Standard Version of the Bible*, John W. Ellison, ed., Thomas Nelson & Sons (New York, 1957), pp. 561-565.

Jesus Christ used the word "evil" frequently, and most often in the narrow, moral sense (e.g., "The good person brings good things out of a good treasure, and the evil person brings evil things out of an evil treasure"—Matthew 12:35; and "It is what comes out of a person that defiles. For it is from within, from the human heart, that evil intentions come: fornication, theft, murder, adultery, avarice, wickedness, deceit, licentiousness, envy, slander, pride, folly. All these evil things come from within, and they defile a person"—Mark 7:20-23).

According to the *Dictionary of the Bible*, both the broad and the narrow senses of the word are used in the Bible:

> The concept is not easily made precise in Biblical thought, for it is hard to distinguish between what we would call sin on one hand and what we would call disaster on the other.[8]

Old Testament references tend, however, more toward the broad sense of the term than do those of the New Testament.[9] *The Interpreter's Dictionary of the Bible* also notes the employment of the broad sense of the word "evil" in the Old Testament: "'[E]vil' means the 'trouble,' 'distress,' and 'calamity' which mankind, and particularly Israel, must endure."[10] This is true even for the "evil" that was "punishment or chastisement sent from God"; because while that in a way suggests the narrower use of the word in a moral context, the real "cause" of that harm was the evil of those receiving the punishment as a consequence of their own transgressions. In the New Testament, by contrast, "evil" has a predominantly moral (and spiritual) connotation. It is there understood as the wrong that men do to each other and the "moral badness, maliciousness and perversity of the sinful heart."[11]

---

8. James Hastings, ed., Charles Scribner's Sons (New York, 1963), p. 277.
9. *Ibid.*
10. George Arthur Buttrick, ed., Abingdon Press (New York, 1962), p. 182.
11. Buttrick (183).

The *International Standard Bible Encyclopedia*[12] states that "evil" has both an "expressive" and a "descriptive" component. Sometimes, when it is expressive of disapproval, that component dominates the meaning of the word (e.g., "This also is vanity and a great evil"—Ecclesiastes 2:21). Its descriptive component is reflected in a variety of conditions: unhappiness (e.g., "All the days of the afflicted are evil"—Proverbs 15:15); harm or threat of harm (e.g., God would bring evil on them if they transgressed the covenant—Joshua 23:15); dysfunction (e.g., "The bad tree bears evil fruit"—Matthew 7:17); or immorality and unfaithfulness to God (e.g., doing "what was evil in the sight of God"—1 Kings 11:6). In the last sense, evil is said to include not only external actions but also internal dispositions:

> This movement from calling actions evil to calling individuals and groups evil seems to be licensed when people habitually do evil, when they stubbornly persist in evil, adamantly refusing education and repentance.[13]

The concept of evil also exists, of course, in other widely practiced religions of the world and is examined and utilized in Hindu, Buddhist and Islamic thought.

According to S. Cromwell Crawford in *The Evolution of Hindu Ethical Ideals*,[14] the moral concept of "evil" in Hindu texts has a long tradition and consists, on the one hand, of doing specific bad things (e.g., in the Vedic Period, the gods were said to inflict men with "the six evils of sleep, sluggishness, anger, hunger, love of gambling and love of women"),[15] and on the other hand, of failing the gods (e.g., through the contradiction of the will of the gods, according to the *Rig Veda*, or through deviation from sacrificial rectitude, according to the *Brahmanas*).[16] Thus, in the sacred texts of the Hindu religion, the narrower moral sense of "evil" appears to

---

12. Bromiley (206-207).
13. Bromiley (207).
14. Firma K.L. Mukhopadhyay (Calcutta, 1974).
15. Crawford (28).
16. Crawford (59).

predominate. However, the proper response to evil in Hindu thought includes not only its opposition but also its complete vanquishment from personal life by the aspirant's attainment of a level of spiritual development that is said to exist beyond morality. In the Upanishads, evil arises out of the mistaken notion that "Reality" is finite and hence from the false consciousness of individuality which alienates man from man and man from nature:

> When the supreme knowledge of the Atman[17] is realized, the individual is transported beyond the ethical plane to the religious plane.... On this level one is not only beyond evil, but beyond the good, for the one presupposes the other.[18]

Padmasiri de Silva wrote that "Buddhist ethics deal both with the nature of the evil states which darken the mind" as well as the wholesome ones which illumine it.[19] He listed sixteen defilements from the sutta on the *Simili of the Cloth* (including greed, covetousness, malevolence, anger, malice, hypocrisy, spite, envy, stinginess, deceit, treachery, obstinacy, impetuosity, arrogance, pride and conceit) as well as "the tenfold evil actions." The latter include "killing, stealing, enjoying sensual pleasures of a wrong nature, false speech, slanderous speech and frivolous talk, as well as intense greed, malevolence and wrong view."[20] Martin Southwold, on the other hand, in "Buddhism and Evil,"[21] described his study of Buddhist works on the concept of evil in the context of his contemporary fieldwork in Sri Lanka. He concluded that the Buddhist concept of evil did not involve as strong a moral component as is the case in Western thinking. He also found that the term "evil" was used less frequently in the strong ethical sense in Buddhism, but more often in the broad, Old Testament sense. However, Southwold

---

17. The *Atman* is defined as the "universal soul."
18. Crawford (72).
19. "Buddhist Ethics," *A Companion to Ethics*, Peter Singer, ed., Blackwell Publishers Ltd. (Oxford, 1993), p. 64.
20. *Ibid.*
21. *The Anthropology of Evil*, David Parkin, ed., Basil Blackwell (Oxford, 1985).

also wrote that under the doctrine of *karma*, "all one's afflictions are the consequences of one's own former misdeeds,"[22] which certainly implies both causation and blame. Nonetheless, he felt that the strong moral sense of the term that attaches to the most heinous wrongs in the West simply does not exist as a concept in Buddhism. Furthermore, while the Buddhist mythological figure Mara is often called "the Evil One" and compared to Satan in the Judeo-Christian tradition, and regarded as a destroyer and a tempter, Southwold believed him to be a disregarded and archaic figure in modern Buddhism. He also suggested that the relative absence of the moral construal of evil among Buddhists follows within a more tolerant group of people who are aware of the internal origins of their own evil and who are more readily inclined to forgive those who do bad things.

The Islamic concept of evil is, of course, tied closely to the Koranic teachings. Islamic law distinguishes between good and bad actions by providing a detailed analysis of them and categorizing them. Three of the categories of human actions concern bad things: acts that are categorically forbidden (such as murder, adultery, blasphemy, theft, intoxication, and so forth), acts that are disapproved of (although there are some exceptions), and acts not permitted in formal worship (e.g., eating during a period of fasting).[23] Two major Muslim theological traditions (the Sunni and the Mu'tazila) have argued strenuously over whether good and evil could be defined rationally or whether distinctions between good and evil must always ultimately come from God. For the dominant school (which takes the latter position), "Acts and obligations were good and evil ultimately because divine commands defined them as such," so those believers have to look to textural direction in the Koran and prophetic tradition.[24]

We can conclude from the sacred texts of the major religions that while evil may have been and may sometimes still be construed in the broad sense of the term, it is now more commonly employed in its narrower sense of immoral harm.

---

22.   Southwold (133).
23.   Azim Nanjii, "Islamic Ethics," *A Companion to Ethics* (113).
24.   Nanji (107, 112).

Prominent Judeo-Christian theologians have provided further analysis of the meaning and nature of evil. St. Augustine defined "evil" as the absence of good, probably in part because this was a key element in his proposed solution to the problem of evil, namely that God created only good but gave people free will, and, for this reason, we can and—unfortunately—do choose non-good where good should be; and therefore that *we* can be said to be responsible for the existence of evil. While the definition of evil as "the absence of good" may be an essentially accurate one, derivative and negative definitions are almost never as satisfying or as helpful as positive and direct ones. Consider, for example, the following: "Black is the absence of color," "A chair is not a couch," or "A dog is not a cat." Perhaps more directly analogous would be "Mendacity is the absence of truth-telling," or "Selfishness is the absence of charity." Is it not clear that we can define all of these examples better when we state their meanings in positive terms? In addition, while it may be accurate to observe that evil is the privation of good, it would be just as logical and consistent to say that good is the absence of evil (as far as both of those statements go); but we would not thereby have advanced significantly in our understanding of the meaning and nature of either term. The construal of evil as the privation of good therefore appears to be incomplete and insufficient. All we have done is make the observation that the continuum of good and evil has two endpoints, and that they are moral opposites.

St. Anselm distinguished between the broad and the narrow definitions of evil. The former he called evil-that-is-detriment, such as pain, and the latter, evil-that-is-injustice, meaning "privation." His use of the term "privation" emphasizes both his belief that moral evil results from a lack of uprightness in the human will and his belief that only such a deficiency is "evil per se."[25]

Thomas Aquinas agreed with Augustine that evil is the privation of goodness and that evil takes its meaning from what is lacking.

---

25. Jasper Hopkins, "Saint Anselm," *The Encyclopedia of Ethics,* Lawrence C. Becker, ed., Garland Publishing, Inc. (New York, 1992), vol. 1, p. 46.

Aquinas also thought, however, that ultimately the good may in some sense explain or even "justify" evil, for the possibility of evil allows many goods to occur (e.g., "If there were no persecution from tyrants, there would be no occasion for the heroic suffering of martyrs").[26] Nikolai Berdyaev evidently concurred, for he believed that evil is the price that humanity has to pay for the actualization of the good.[27] My principal reaction to all of these negative approaches to the definition of evil, however, is that they have not shown that a positive definition of it is not possible, nor have they demonstrated that a positive definition would not be helpful.

Martin Buber wrote that evil is the lack or loss not of good, but rather of direction, and that evil occurs when the I-It relation dominates our lives, instead of the I-Thou relation that accompanies good.[28] He did not agree that good and evil share the same continuum, because of their disparate natures:

> Good and evil ... cannot be a pair of opposites like left and right or above and beneath. "Good" is the movement in the direction of home, "evil" is the aimless whirl of human potentialities without which nothing can be achieved and by which, if they take

---

26. Vernon J. Bourke, "St. Thomas Aquinas," *The Encyclopedia of Philosophy*, vol. 8, p. 111, quoting from *Summa Theologiae I*, 22,2 ad 2).

27. As put by James W. Dye, "Nikolai Berdyaev," *The Encyclopedia of Philosophy*, vol. 1, p. 287: "Even if history involves failure and suffering, its failure is a profound failure and its suffering is justified to the degree that historical beings actualize that nonhistorical community of personal values that is Berdyaev's equivalent of the Kingdom of God." See also *The Meaning of Evil*, Charles Journet, trans. Michael Barry, P. J. Kenedy & Sons (New York, 1963), pp. 98-99, in which the author wrote that both Berdyaev and Dostoyevsky concluded that "Evil, suffered in humility, is the price humanity has to pay for greatness."

28. *Evil and Suffering in Jewish Philosophy*, Oliver Leaman, Cambridge University Press (1995), p. 168.

no direction but remain trapped in themselves, everything goes awry.[29]

Buber's comments appear to focus more on the psychology of evil, however—on why we do it and on its consequences for us—than on the intrinsic nature of the term itself. He sought to emphasize his positions on those issues in the passage cited above by attempting to redefine good and evil; but I would argue that his attempted redefinition essentially fails, because we continue generally to accept the contrariety of good and evil and because we have been presented with no convincing reason not to do so; and, in any event, if home is the direction of good, evil directionlessness would still be its opposite.

Another theological approach to evil posits that it is "separation from God." If God is good (as Judeo-Christian believers hold), then separation from the good would, like privation of good, be a valid aspect of a full definition of evil. However, in my view, "separation from God" is more a cause and a consequence of evil than a definition or an explanation of its nature. Also, "separation from God" does not in and of itself help us identify particular things or acts as evil. For that, we need either religious instruction on what exactly "separations from God" are (e.g., doing acts that God has commanded us not to do) or a more specific understanding of the concept of evil. While religious instruction can provide us with directions about acts which are to be avoided, the second of these alternatives, namely the search for a definition of evil, might still be of assistance to us in our attempt to discern why certain things are evil and, as a consequence, why those things may separate us from God.

Much religious instruction about evil corresponds essentially to our general secular conceptions of it, in its narrow and morally-based sense. Nevertheless, on many occasions our religious and secular characterizations of particular manifestations of evil are not in conformity. It can be interesting to consider whether, over time,

---

29. *Ibid.*, quoting from *Between Man and Men*, Routledge Kegan and Paul (London, 1949), (78).

religions tend to adapt to such a divergence or whether the underlying general concepts of evil themselves tend to change.

Philosophers have also studied and analyzed evil, but, as noted above, it has rarely been a primary focus in their writings on ethics. Most philosophers are more interested in what we should seek than in what we should avoid. Hence, Socrates, Plato and Aristotle concentrated more on virtue and on the good, happiness and justice than on evil (although Plato wrote that it is not possible for evils to be destroyed because something must always remain "opposite to the good"[30]).

Leibniz distinguished among metaphysical evil, physical evil and moral evil. He thought that metaphysical evil was found in lack of perfection,[31] while physical evil involved the broad use of the term (the suffering of sentient beings, without a necessary moral element). Moral evil was sin, which he called the violation of universal jurisprudence by moral agents.[32]

Immanuel Kant wrote that evil actions are impossible to explain, although he suggested that the source of evil is our "sensible nature." He thought that a "radical evil" exists in human nature because we have a propensity to evil, which is expressed in frailty (in our failure to act toward the good), in impurity, and in wickedness.[33] On the other hand, he also denied "that the human will can be 'malignant' or take evil itself as an incentive." [34]

Arthur Schopenhauer held that those who are ethical are able to recognize the common unitary nature shared by all things, and that evil actions stem from the egoism that resists and opposes this

---

30. *Theaetetus,* 176; trans. John McDowell, Clarendon Press (Oxford, 1973), p. 53.

31. Cf. the privation of good.

32. R. C. Sleigh, Jr., "Gottfried Wilhelm Leibniz," *Encyclopedia of Ethics*, vol. 2, p. 692.

33. Christine M. Korsgaard, "Immanuel Kant," *Encyclopedia of Ethics*, vol. 1, pp. 669.

34. *Ibid.* (669-670).

insight.[35] He believed that those who discern the illusory character of the phenomenal world draw less pronounced distinctions between themselves and others, and thus are less likely to try to manipulate and dominate others.

Among contemporary philosophers, John Kekes described primary and derivative senses of the word in *Facing Evil*.[36] In its "primary" sense, "evil" refers to "the undeserved harm human beings cause one another and themselves." "Derivative" evil occurs when "there has been a pattern of primary evil that can reasonably be attributed to a character trait, person, practice, group or institution." He also described a difference between "simple evil" (which deprives people of the minimum requirements of their welfare) and "complex evil" (which involves things that go beyond those minimum requirements and derive from particular conceptions of good lives, which are historically, culturally and individually variable).[37]

One can be deemed culpable for an evil act in three different ways, according to Ronald Milo. The harm-inflictor may be acting intentionally; he may be acting habitually or almost automatically in accordance with a character defect or a vice that he possesses; or he may be acting negligently.[38]

Finally, the meaning of the word "evil" is also conveyed by its use in the mass media and popular culture. "Evil" is often employed in the media when major damage has been purposefully caused for what the speaker or writer believes are totally inadequate or inappropriate reasons. The Oklahoma City bombing in 1995 was quickly referred to as an "evil act." When children are horribly hurt or killed by deranged individuals, the word "evil" is commonly

35. Rudolf Malter, "Arthur Schopenhauer," *Encyclopedia of Ethics*, vol. 2, p. 1129; Patrick Gardiner, "Arthur Schopenhauer," *The Encyclopedia of Philosophy*, vol. 7, p. 331.
36. Princeton University Press (1990), pp. 47-49.
37. Kekes (51-53).
38. *Immorality*, Ronald D. Milo, Princeton University Press (1984), pp. 82-114; see also Kekes, *Facing Evil*.

heard. Random destruction and injury to the innocent and vulnerable are thus two types of action which are often labeled with the word "evil" in our news stories and commentaries.

The individuals and groups who have perpetrated these kinds of horrific events are frequently called "evil" as well. The adjective is applied in histories to the leaders of groups or countries that have committed massive atrocities, including Caligula and Nero in ancient Rome and Hitler and Stalin in the modern era. "Evil" is sometimes attributed to larger groups as well. Consider, for example, the label "evil empire" that was applied to the Soviet Union by Ronald Reagan.

The word "evil" was used approximately two thousand times in a twenty-one-month period in the mid-1990's in *The New York Times*, and a review of those articles demonstrates the preponderance of the narrow use of the word (in its morally-based sense) and the near obsolescence of its use in the older, broader sense. Terms like "evil manipulators," "evil aunts," and "evil twins" overwhelmed the articles' isolated references to evil which neither contained nor implied a moral element.[39]

A good deal of our entertainment industry employs or exploits the basic and perennial theme of good against evil. "Evil" is frequently depicted in literature, and particularly in fiction, whether the medium is print or film. Fiction has also provided countless evil villains whom we can revile, from Captain Ahab to Lady Macbeth and from Captain Hook to Darth Vadar. Numerous nonfiction works also directly or indirectly address the issue of evil, insofar as they often first describe things that the authors believe to be terribly wrong and then propose solutions to them. Consider, for example, Rachel Carson's *Silent Spring*, Ralph Nader's *Unsafe at Any Speed*, and Thomas Paine's *Common Sense*.

As this brief survey shows, and as might be expected, our social and cultural traditions have provided various approaches to and

---

39. Data search of the word, "evil," *The New York Times*, January, 1996-September, 1997.

perspectives on the meaning of the word "evil," even when it is construed only in the narrow, morally-based sense of the term. Many of these comments and observations, however, are consistent with each other and thus suggest that there is fairly wide agreement on the basic use of the concept. The next chapter will outline an approach to the definition of "evil" that I believe to be appropriate given this foundation. That approach will subsequently be employed in discussions of the tasks of identifying and confronting evil and other forms of immorality.

2

THE ESSENTIAL ELEMENTS
OF EVIL

The dictionary definitions of evil in its morally-based sense (e.g., "immoral," "wicked," "sinful," "malicious") provide us with its general direction and some useful synonyms, but they do not constitute a serious effort to understand its nature and identify its manifestations. They tell us that certain conduct, thoughts or people may be censurable; but to comprehend more fully what evil is and when and how the word should be used, we need to know much more about it.

A number of other approaches to an understanding of the word "evil" do not aid us considerably in these efforts, either. Many of them simply describe certain types or instances of evil. Pointing out examples of something does not, however, explain its intrinsic nature, just as pointing out examples of chairs (e.g., an easy chair or a recliner) does not sufficiently explain what a chair is. While this method may succeed in its objective of branding certain acts, persons or thoughts as reprehensible, it does not tell us how—other than by analogy—to recognize other types and examples of evil. Rather, the word "evil" is simply being used in exhortations to avoid, minimize and oppose certain acts, persons or thoughts. Using the word "evil" in this manner is often a precursor to action; it is a powerful expression which is employed to induce certain attitudes and commitments to action, often in opposition to something. Many calls to arms include disparagements of the enemy as part of an effort to build up a righteous fervor, and one of the most effective ways to belittle an enemy is to call him (or her, them or it) "evil." Recalling the items on the lists of things that are being so castigated can help us understand, in incremental terms, what others believe evil to be; but a more basic analysis is still possible and could help reveal what all of those examples and lists may have in common.

Similarly, collections of general observations on the origin of evil (as opposed to the origin of specific evil acts, such as the envy that produces a murder) are of equally limited value in this endeavor. Whether the ultimate source of evil is considered to be original sin, separation from God, the ego, a failure of understanding, or—as is perhaps more often suggested in our times—bad genes or childhood social or economic deprivation, none of these proposed explanations helps us very much in identifying evil itself or in understanding its essential nature. Even though our understanding of evil is expanded when we know its causes, we still must look elsewhere to fully grasp its nature and to obtain the necessary practical help in identifying its various manifestations.

Another approach discussed in the previous chapter focused on derivative definitions. To be able to use such a definition of evil (e.g., "the privation of good"), we must not only possess and be able to apply a basic knowledge of the main definition (e.g., of what is good), but also know when the derivative definition should be used (e.g., when a "privation" occurs or when the good is otherwise lacking). If we look at any evil act in isolation, we can clearly see that it occurs in a situation in which some kind of good is absent; but at the same time, it also helps if we understand what is present. Before we try to define something in exclusively negative terms (e.g., "evil is 'not-good'"), we ought to try to find out whether a more direct approach to the definition is possible (in this case, by seeking an adequate, positive definition of "evil"). If so, then in many situations, the straightforward definition may be more useful.

The concept of "evil" contains several different essential elements. Most often, the first major question that we face is whether something harmful has happened, is happening, or is impending. In other words, the first discernible element of evil is the presence of something that causes some injury or does some damage. The second element which comes to the fore in our analysis is the idea of an agent; we need to ask whether anyone is, was or would be responsible for causing the harm. In cases in which there is no identifiable moral agent, it can only be said that an unfortunate accident has occurred, and not that a moral wrong has been perpetrated. Innocent harmfulness (which occurs, for example, when a small child, running from a suddenly barking dog, accidentally bumps into her father and causes a parental bruise) cannot be labeled "evil" or "wrong." The third element of our analysis is the question of whether or not there is any justification for the harm. We live in a world where there is much pain and hurt, but not all of those pains and hurts are the result of "evil" (in the narrow morally-based sense of the term). Sometimes, for example, there is nothing morally wrong with "harm" for which we are responsible, as when we move a splinter around while removing it from a finger or make a child feel bad during a scolding for having played with matches.

If all three of these elements are present in a given situation, then we can call the act or event "morally wrong" and possibly "evil," and we can consider the responsible party culpable. In other words, we do evil when we are responsible for causing harm that is not justified.

Each of these three major elements needs to be present to some degree before we can correctly label something as "evil." Conversely, if one or more of these elements are missing, we do not and will not call an action or event evil, but rather something else (e.g., an unfortunate accident). Therefore, I suggest the following as a working definition of "evil" in the morally-based sense of the term: (1) a harmful act (2) for which someone is responsible and (3) for which there is no adequate moral justification. The first and second elements of this analysis (whether something is harmful and whether someone was responsible for causing the harm) are largely matters of fact and factual characterization (even though a number of valuations may be involved). The third element, which involves justice and injustice, is primarily a matter of moral judgment.

As with most lists and systems of categories, what is being proposed here is not the only way in which to identify or characterize the essential elements of an important concept like evil. In some situations, for example, it might be useful to expand the list to include eight elements:

1. An action
2. affecting a person (or an object)
3. who was harmed thereby;

and:

4. the harm which was caused
5. was the result of acts or omissions
6. of a specific person or persons
7. who were responsible for it;

and finally:

8. the harm was not justified.

The three-step test set out in the previous paragraph compresses some additional fact issues (items (1) through (7) in the longer list) which may be important in some cases. We do not routinely need to determine whether or not an action occurred, however, because harm is almost always a consequence of some action or event. Nevertheless, on some occasions, doing so might provide a missing detail that exonerates a person wrongly accused of perpetrating some evil action. In other words, sometimes awareness of the nuances involved in the description of a situation can make a difference. While the three-element list proposed here may not explicitly identify all of the issues involved in determining whether evil is present in a given circumstance, it does adequately describe its most important and indispensable elements. I will therefore be taking this approach in the analysis of evil which follows.

The Element of Harm

"Harm" is some kind of injury—something that hurts, damages or is detrimental in some way to someone or to some thing. It is interesting that this first element of "moral evil" coincides roughly with what we have previously been calling the "broad definition" of evil, in which evil is identified solely with that which is harmful or causes suffering. This also helps us to better place the morally-based definition of evil in its appropriate context: it is essentially "harm-plus," or harm plus some other elements. Furthermore, it suggests that while the concept of "evil" may originally have been used to describe all of the bad things that happened to us (perhaps with a belief that most bad things were directly caused by bad spirits of some sort), as time passed and as we gained knowledge not only of causation generally but also of the more specific causes of many things, and as we further distinguished between morally neutral causes and malevolent ones, the moral aspect of the definition came into play.

There are many varieties of harm, and it can occur in many settings. It can be done to individuals or to groups; it can be directed toward certain targets; it can happen to innocent bystanders; and it can even happen to perpetrators or their collaborators. We can cause harm to other forms of life (animals or plants); we can also cause harm to specific objects, to collections of objects, or to ecosystems of objects. Indeed, we can cause harm to the entire world. Some-times, even though an action may cause direct and immediate harm to one or several specific objects, it sets in motion a sort of wave of destructive or injurious effects; then harm spreads progressively to others not originally intended as its objects. Furthermore, we need to note that, while we can usually cause harm by engaging in a given action, we can also cause it by failing or neglecting to perform some action. Harm may come in the form of a blow to the body, for example, or it may result from the failure to strike a blow in response to a given threat. Some harm is perceived immediately, and some gradually; but some may also go unperceived indefinitely. Harm may occur concurrently with the act which causes it, or its effect may be delayed.

Harm can be perceived in several different ways. When we think of it, what first comes to mind is usually physical injury and pain. Pain is a sensation in response to physical harm. We know pain when we feel it—the body and mind react immediately. But we also frequently suffer only mentally, as we experience, for example, the pain of the loss of a loved one.

While pain may be a good starting point for analyzing harm, it is not adequate by itself. Immediate pain does not accompany all harm, and some forms of harm simply are not accompanied by what we traditionally sense to be pain. For example, we can be harmed politically, economically or socially—indeed, we can be harmed in terms of every type of endeavor or activity that we may undertake. We can be harmed when we receive things (e.g., a bad apple) or when we are deprived of things (e.g., air).

To understand better what it is that makes something harmful to us, we need to understand human needs and wants. If we can identify certain basic and common forms of these, we should be able to more precisely determine what constitutes harm to human beings; because harm often comes to us when we are prevented from meeting or fulfilling our needs and wants.

An excellent starting point for a discussion of different types of human needs and wants is Abraham Maslow's hierarchically ranged list.[1] It begins with the basic physiological needs for air, water, food, shelter, sleep and sex, moves to higher needs, including safety and security, love and a feeling of belonging, self-esteem and esteem from others, and finally, ends with self-actualization. One of the ways in which we can identify harm is by determining whether someone is being prevented from fulfilling or hindered in their efforts to fulfill any of these needs. We are harmed when we are deprived, for example, of food or sleep or security or love.

Many of our "wants" are directly related to our "needs" but go beyond the latter's satisfaction. We want the specific kinds of food and shelter that we consider desirable, for example, and not merely the minimal sustenance and refuge that would keep us alive. And, since our wants and needs may parallel each other in many ways, we are often aware of how we can be harmed insofar as we observe how something affects our interests as they are outlined on Maslow's list of needs.

We can take yet another approach to recognizing harm by determining whether something moves us toward what I refer to as the "negative ground of being." In *Being Ethical* I wrote of the

---

1. *Motivation and Personality*, 2d ed., Harper & Row (New York, 1970).

positive ground of being, which helps us validate morality (because doing what is right tends to move us in the direction of the positive things in life).[2] But there exists also a negative one, which consists of the bad directions that we can take and the bad places that we can visit or inhabit. Included in the group of conditions that make up the negative ground of being are such things as unhappiness, dissatisfaction, failure, rejection, captivity, death, bad feelings, retrogression, pain, absence of pleasure, ill-health, ignorance, isolation, alienation, hate, disharmony, war, instability, irrationality, atrophy, and so on. Anything that moves us toward any of the elements of the negative ground of being can also fairly be called "harm." Hence, whatever leads us into or moves us toward, for example, war, ill-health, pain or failure causes us harm.

Evil begins with harm or with impending harm. There are several different ways in which we can determine and confirm that something is harmful. The "harm" element of evil is present not only when we sense pain in ourselves or others but also when we see that something has had an injurious impact on someone's needs and wants, or that an action or event is leading toward the negative ground of being. If something has had, is having, or would have an impact of this sort on us, we can call it "harmful" and establish the presence of the first of the three elements of evil.

The Element of Responsibility for the Harm

Responsibility for harm can be analyzed in terms of two main issues, the first being whether the person in question actually caused the harm, and the second being whether that person could have avoided causing the harm. We need to take into consideration the fact that someone who causes an unjust harm to another person may not be responsible for his or her actions for one reason or another. In other words, responsibility must be established before we can determine culpability. Only if we find that a person actually caused harm to another, and only if that person could also have avoided it,

---

2. Kroshka Books (Commack, NY, 1999), pp. 107-109.

are we able to proceed toward a conclusion that something evil has happened.

In order to hold someone responsible for an evil, he or she will first have to have been the one who actually *caused* the harm to occur. We understand causation by observing how the world works. All of our overt actions, and many of our conscious omissions, have direct consequences: if we do A, B occurs; if we do not do X, then Y will happen. In other words, we know that if we do (or neglect to do) something, our action (or inaction) will have a direct effect on and a determinable consequence for something else.

Many causes are clear to us, yet others are not. I am causing ink to be applied to paper as I write; but what caused a sound I heard outside just now is not apparent. Fortunately, a number of causes can be ascertained with a little investigation. ("Aha! Looking out my window I see a dog sniffing around an overturned garbage can; the dog must have made the noise.") Still other causes can only be identified after a great deal of investigation. In some cases, our investigations are inconclusive; and occasionally, they provide us with no real clues as to the causes of a given event.

Investigating causes and drawing conclusions about them, however, is part of everyday life and something at which we must become fairly adept in order to get along in this world, particularly in the relatively complex one that we now inhabit. We have to reason often that "If I do A, then B will occur," and to understand that "There's a B, therefore someone must have done A."

Even when the other essential elements of evil are present—unjustified harm having been done to a person or an object and an agent who would be culpable if he had indeed caused it—we are still obligated to prove both the identity of the perpetrator and a cause and effect relation between his or her actions and the outcome. Bad intentions do not, in and of themselves, constitute an evil act; rather, something specific must be done (or omitted) that leads to or imminently threatens to bring about actual harm before an evil action can be said to have occurred.[3]

---

3. Bad intentions, or bad thoughts, may be described as culpable in the sense of their propensity to lead us into bad conduct. Nevertheless, they do not become events which are injurious to others in the

The concept of "proximate cause" has been developed in tort law under common law traditions to address this issue. If someone is to be held legally responsible for an injury to another, his or her act (or omission) must have been the direct cause of the injury under discussion, and also there can have been no effective intervening causes. Thus, while Driver A may have "caused" Driver B to become angry by driving on the wrong side of the road so that Driver B had to swerve to avoid Driver A, Driver A did not *cause* Driver B to plow into the back of Driver C's car two minutes later, even though Driver B may still have been reacting with anger to Driver A's prior negligent act. The same concept is applicable in our analysis of the cause or causes of evil; it should only be deemed to be present if the act (or the omission) of the one whom we would otherwise hold culpable for the unjustified harm did in fact directly cause that harm.

Often the facts about causation are apparent and undisputed, and it is clear that one person's actions are what caused harm to another. But frequently the facts are either unclear because they are unknown (or only partially known), because they are jumbled or obscured, or because we are being deceived about them. Most people who intend to do evil things (especially when they also break the law) try to hide the fact that they caused the harm, denying it at every turn and planting red herrings wherever they can. And where a causal connection has not been clearly and directly established, we have to proceed on the basis of the best information available to us; and that information may only provide circumstantial support for our conclusion. Experience, context and reasoned analysis sometimes help us through these issues when they are muddled; but in order to conclude that some evil action or event has occurred, we must determine definitely that some person has caused the harm. And if we want to determine that a specific person has done something evil, we have to be able to conclude that the person who is suspected of it has actually been the cause of the harm.

The analysis of the second issue in this element of responsibility, namely, the capacity to avoid causing the harm, is carried out in two-

---

absence of actual actions.

steps. First, we need to determine whether the person causing the harm knew or should have known that the act that caused the harm would or was likely to cause such harm. Second, we need to look at whether the person who caused the harm had the mental and physical capability not to do the act that caused the harm. If a person who actually caused the harm knew or should have known that his action would cause or was likely to cause harm and if that person also could have avoided that action, then he or she should be held responsible for the act that caused the harm.

When we consider causation by itself, we usually focus on a sequence of observable events. Did finger A actually push button B that led to consequence C? If we identify such a progression, then we can claim that there exists a causal connection between agent, action and outcome. When we have to consider the capacity of the agent for avoiding a given action, however, we must look primarily at internal factors. What we can conclude about the mental activities of the one causing the harm? What did he know (or should he have known) at the time of the harmful act, and could he have avoided engaging in the action if he had wanted to do so? To correctly identify this second aspect of responsibility for a harmful act we must be able to conclude that: (1) the actor was capable of having certain types of knowledge; (2) he was aware or should have known about the potentially harmful consequences of the act in question; (3) he was generally capable of controlling his own actions; and (4) he could have avoided engaging in the specific action that ended up having harmful consequences.

If we are to possess, or to have ascribed to us, the type of knowledge that makes us responsible for our own actions, we need both a certain level of general knowledge (e.g., awareness of cause and effect relations) and also a fairly extensive repertoire of specific, experiential knowledge (e.g., the practical understanding of the consequences of physical actions such as hitting someone's nose). Some people are incapable of developing the fund of general knowledge which would render them responsible for their particular actions. This is what exculpates one-year-olds and some schizophrenics who engage in actions which lead to unjust harm. If they did not understand the consequences of their actions, and if we know that they could not have understood them, then we should not and will not hold them responsible for their actions, no matter what the harmful consequences may have been. We try to protect others from them (and to protect them from themselves); but if an action for which someone is not responsible sets in motion a sequence of events that lead to an unjust harm, we will not call the action "evil," but rather will describe the outcome as an "unfortunate accident."

The same thing is true of knowledge or the attribution of knowledge of specific causes or consequences. Even if someone understands causation, if that person has no reason to believe that a given act may lead to a harmful consequence, then we should not find the actor liable for those consequences. Decisions of this sort should be made cautiously, because we generally know how the world works, and hence "should have known" about the potentially dangerous consequences of most specific actions. We often can (or should be able to) sense when we are in risky situations, and we should therefore also be able to assess when it is necessary to reason about the possible consequences of any actions we are planning. That is, the notion that we "should have known" draws us into the realm of moral responsibility even though we may truly be unaware of the danger at the time we are contemplating some action. But, in some circumstances, even a normally prudent person could not possibly discern that a specific type of act would be likely to have a harmful consequence; and, in such cases, the actor cannot be judged morally responsible for the unjustified harm.

To hold someone responsible for a given action, we also need to know whether or not he is able to control his own actions. In general, if we can control our actions, then we can justifiably be held responsible for them—even when we do not happen to exercise sufficient control over them. On the other hand, if a person is genuinely incapable of controlling his own actions (e.g., someone afflicted with Parkinson's disease), and something he does causes unjust harm to another, that person would not be considered culpable.

Finally, there is the question of circumstances which are external to the will of the actor that limit or somehow condition his choices. In other words, even if a person is generally in control of his actions, we still may need to determine whether he really could have avoided performing (or not performing) some action. In most cases, action is not coerced, and the will is free.[4] When we turn to the left at an intersection, we usually could have proceeded in other directions as well. In some situations, however, the actor may have had no other choice than to perform the action that led to unjust harm, and hence should not be held responsible for the consequences. This may apply in cases where we are being coerced into doing something by others, but sometimes there are also clearly physical conditions which impose limits on our choices (e.g., when our only option at a street corner is to turn left).

Culpability is negative moral responsibility which is assigned to an agent who engages in immoral actions. If we know or should know that an action that we might take could cause unjust harm and if we have the ability to either carry out the act or not to do so, and we then go ahead and do it, we are responsible for both the act and the subsequent unjust harm, and consequently we are appropriately characterized as culpable.

The Element of the
Lack of Justification for the Harm

Judgments about actions in the domain of ethics can be justified or unjustified; they are either supported by valid moral reasoning and decision-making, or they are not.

When all ethical indicators point in a single direction,[5] we do not normally stop to ponder whether we should proceed in that way; if we want to do what is ethical, we move forward, confident of the rightness of our actions. It is only when we are faced with moral dilemmas that we become concerned with the adequacy of the justifications for our actions.

When we are confronted with a moral dilemma—when we recognize that there are good moral reasons to do something and good moral reasons not to do it—we are forced to reason about our choices (unless we are willing to accept an unnecessary moral paralysis, which eventually becomes an unethical state in and of

---

4. Or, at the very least, we have to act as if we have free will.
5. That is, when they are in ethical harmony.

itself). This process of seeking to justify our actions consists of several steps. First, we seek and identify, to the extent possible, the valid moral arguments that are applicable to the circumstance; and secondly, we attempt to support our arguments and also to challenge them. Then we conclude that our contemplated action either is or is not morally justified. This process is necessary in any situation in which there are apparently legitimate moral arguments which point in either direction.

When we are primarily concerned with determining whether something is evil or otherwise morally wrong, it is usually because there are already some very good reasons to suspect that this is the case. Indeed, we normally think about the moral justification of a judgment about evil only when a *prima facie* case of evil has been presented to us (such a *prima facie* case being one in which the first two elements of evil are present—i.e., when harm has been done and someone is responsible for it, and when there is no obvious reason to think that the third element will not also be present). We can term this a *prima facie* case because causing harm is always wrong if it is done without adequate justification, given two of our general benevolence duties—not to do harm to others and not to cause injustice to them.

But frequently we *do* have to consider other factors in our ethical decision-making process. This is primarily because the multiple approaches we take in reasoning about moral choices can lead to the conclusion that sometimes and in some contexts, doing "harm" is ethically justified. Indeed, in some situations, causing "harm" may even be ethically required, even though absent such justifications, it would clearly be wrong to cause the harm. In order to understand and have confidence in those justifications, we have to identify and articulate these issues, and to weigh and balance them.

Virtually all valid ethical objectives can provide justifications for causing some type of harm when they are juxtaposed against each other. From time to time, for example, it is appropriate to suffer hunger pangs in order to finish work by a deadline (despite a normal moral goal of avoiding pain in a reasonable manner), because doing so may be required either by a duty of fidelity or one of self-realization (or both).

When we attempt to justify doing harm, it is helpful first to consider the matter solely from the perspective of the "victim," and then, if that does not resolve it, to take a look at whether any possibly moral interests of others may be involved. The two basic models of justification that proceed along these lines are:

(1) While this specific harm would be bad for this victim, it would be appropriate because it is what he deserves for something that he has done that is wrong, because he needs to learn that it is wrong, or because it would on balance bring some benefit or good to the victim himself that outweighs the harm; or

(2) While this harm would be bad for this victim, it would on balance be good because of a benefit or good accruing to a different person or group of people that outweighs the harm to the victim.

This justification process is how we make—and must make—valid but difficult moral judgments. In order to identify evil, it is necessary that we first determine that the object of the harm does *not* deserve it and that it would not, for some other reason, be unjust to him or her. Finally, we have to rule out the justifications that may also need to be taken into account when we expand the considerations to include the consequences of the action or actions for others.

Harm is considered to be justified when it is deserved, and we deserve something when we have earned it—when something we have done merits our getting something for it. We usually deserve good things when we have done good things,[6] but we can also deserve bad things (e.g., harmful punishments) when we have done bad things.[7] Harm may be inflicted upon us in return for bad

---

6. Although in order to earn ethical credit, we would also need good intent; but that often accompanies good deeds, whether from extended deliberation or from the virtually instantaneous responses of a good character.

7. Interestingly, it is more often the case that we are blamed for a harmful act than credited for a beneficial one, because culpability

actions—in part to give us our just deserts for doing something bad, in part to try to correct what may be a developing problem with our character, and in part to prevent both us and others from doing the same bad things again. Harm that is just punishment for a bad act is therefore deserved; and if it is thus deserved, causing that harm would not be a malevolent act, because the third element of evil (the lack of justification for doing the harm to its object) would be missing.

Legitimate self-defense can also lead to our justifiably inflicting harm upon someone. If you are physically attacked and you happen to cause an injury to the person who is assaulting you while defending yourself, your actions will not be labeled "evil" (as long as you were, in fact, attacked, did not respond disproportionately, and so forth). Once again, in such a situation, where harm is inflicted on someone whose own improper actions have provoked it, he or she is deserving of "appropriate" harm they may suffer as a result of a reaction on the part of the victim.

We say that harm is deserved in the context of punishment or self-defense when someone has, by his or her own actions or omissions, "merited" that harm as a direct consequence of those actions or inactions, as they are weighed in keeping with these guidelines. Something he or she has previously done—or a failure to have done something—must have been judged to have been bad or deficient in some respect. Hence, deservedness of some new harm (in the form of punishment or as a result of self-defense) first requires a finding of a prior culpable act or omission by the one who receives the new harm. And such a finding constitutes a moral judgment about either a prior action or failure to act on the part of the intended object of the new harm.

But deserved harm is not the only kind of justifiable harm. Harm done to a "victim" can also be justified when it is actually and clearly done for the *benefit* of the "victim" in some way, when we take into consideration a larger perspective or a longer period of time, or both. One kind of justified harm often occurs when we teach small children (and others)—either for their own benefit or for our

---

may be ascribed to some unintentional but preventable harms, whereas moral praise only attaches to intentionally good acts.

collective social benefit—about things that they need to know when the instruction itself involves something unpleasant (e.g., restriction to a room for a certain period of time). We do not cause unjustified harm when we deprive a child of playtime, for example, when the child needs to do homework. Justified harm in that situation not only is *not* evil, but is also both good *and* ethically required. Making such distinctions is what our fidelity/role relationship duties require of us, as well as our duties to act benevolently. In the context of legitimate instruction, determining when to use a teaching method which can be described as "harmful" requires a broad understanding both of what people need and want and of how best to train them to achieve those goals. However, it also requires either the absence of other effective teaching methods for imparting the same knowledge without harm (or with less harm) or the existence of some imperativeness in the learning situation (e.g., a need for a major safety lesson about busy streets on the spot).

Finally, when we are considering only the "victim's" perspective, harm caused to someone may ultimately be beneficial to them in ways other than the instruction they need for their own well-being or advancement. Frequently harm of some sort is simply an unpleasant price to be paid for the achievement of something that is, on balance, far more beneficial; its presence is more advantageous to the "victim" than its absence would be. In such cases, we can say that the "net" effect to the "victim" is beneficial, and that causing the harm (or undergoing it ourselves) is not unjustified. The injury caused by surgery is, for example, justified by the successful outcome of an operation. The incision still hurts, but the body heals and its overall condition improves. This can hardly be said to be evil. We do not really "deserve" the harm or the hurt when the "harm" is an unpleasant part of a beneficial process; rather, we deserve the positive outcome which can only be obtained by our being subject to a certain amount of suffering.

Thus, in order to find unjustifiable harm from the perspective of the victim, we have to determine both that there was not some prior act for which this person was culpable which warranted a proportionately harmful reprisal and that the harm suffered is not part of a justified intervention which has as its end object the long-term benefit of the "victim." An initial action for which one is deemed culpable or a justified need for a harm that may lead to the direct benefit to the "victim" may legitimately trigger a harmful response of punishment, self-defense, instruction or intervention. And if the harm is so deserved or justified, then the act in question is not part of an evil event because it lacks the third element in this analysis.

The list of the different types of deserved or otherwise justified harm from the perspective of the victim is *not* extensive. Unless such harm is just punishment, legitimate self-defense or appropriate instruction, or unless it is in the personal, longer-term interest of the victim, it is undeserved and otherwise unjustified. And if harm is unjustified, then this portion of the test for evil will have been met.

At this point there remains to be discussed but one other potential justification for harm. It is usually not taken into consideration when reviewing actions by those who inadvertently cause harm (that is, those who do so as a result of negligence), but rather by those who *intentionally* cause harm to others. If the actor causes some harm to the victim which, when viewed solely from the perspective of the victim, is undeserved and unjustified, but the actor does so for a legitimate "higher good," the actor may be exculpated to some degree, or even completely exonerated. This leads us down the slippery slopes of means/ends justifications. On occasion, however, harm which is caused intentionally and which is unjust from the perspective of the victim is considered to have been warranted by consideration of some greater subsequent good for others. The consequence of this is that before we can determine culpability for some harm apparently unjustly done, we may have to eliminate any argument about a "higher good." And because this justification usually only comes into play when we have the "higher goods" in mind (it is difficult to be trying to accomplish a "higher good" inadvertently), this factor is most often only relevant—and usually only needs to be examined—when the actor is intentionally causing the harm. Consider, for example, the minor harm that might happen to a passenger who is shoved out of the way when a security guard pushes by him in order to subdue a hijacker. We simply will not hold the security guard culpable for the slight harm done to that passenger when his action saved a hundred lives in the face of a threat from a madman.

Ultimately, to assign culpability, we have to determine either that the actor lacked any justified purpose for engaging in some action or that the purpose was insufficiently justified. If we determine that the harm was unjustified from the perspective of the victim and if we find that there exists no higher end for anyone else which might legitimate engaging in the contemplated action, then we have found the third element in our analysis—the lack of justification for the harm—to exist.

If this three-part analysis is correct, then in order to call something "evil" in a moral context, we need to determine that some harm was caused to someone by a party who is responsible for it, and that the harm cannot be adequately justified.

If we have accurately identified the relevant components of evil, what can be said about immorality more generally? I would suggest that we can identify (and classify) every kind and degree of immorality by employing this three-element framework for the analysis. Immorality that is not truly evil (i.e., lesser degrees of immorality) is different from evil due to the degree to which each of the elements is present or absent. To conclude that something is immoral, even if it may not be evil, we need to determine that some degree of harm has been incurred, some degree of responsibility can be assigned for it, and some lack of justness characterizes the situation. General immorality involves the same three basic elements as does evil; but it encompasses many more acts and many more situations, because it includes everything that is morally wrong, and not just the most egregious examples of moral wrongs. Methods for distinguishing the most serious and reprehensible immoral acts (evil per se) from the other degrees of immorality on the negative side of the ethical spectrum will be discussed in Chapter 5.

3

RECOGNIZING EVIL

Evil has many faces. While at times it may be open and obvious, evil can also assume a wide variety of disguises. When we are taken in by some evil that has been wrapped into a convincingly innocent disguise, upon discovering the truth about it, we are chagrined at having been so effectively duped.

The effectiveness of its many camouflages is one reason why it is sometimes difficult to recognize evil, especially in the early stages of its development. This is particularly true for the most virulent type of evil. Perpetrators who have the specific intent of engaging in a harmful act know that their chances of "success" increase if they can hide the evil face of their actions as long as they are able to do so, for that will minimize opposition to the accomplishment of their objectives.

We may also have difficulty recognizing a specific instance of evil because one or more of its three elements may not be readily identifiable. There can be a number of reasons for this, including the generally complex nature of life, the occasional ambiguity of our needs, interests and motives, and the evolution of characters and objectives. Many factors may impede our ability to identify harm and responsibility accurately or may interfere with our judgments about justness and unjustness. Furthermore, if the identification of evil, which is the most obvious kind of immorality, can be difficult at times, then the recognition of other "lesser" kinds of immorality can be even more so.

We can become more adept at recognizing evil, however, as we become more knowledgeable about each of the three elements that comprise it. We can increase our ability to recognize evil further by improving our understanding of the process by which we combine our factual and moral determinations about these elements and arrive at conclusions about a potentially evil act, person or thing.

Recognizing the Element of Harm

We usually make judgments about harm immediately. With accumulated experience we build up extensive knowledge about many types of things that have harmed us in the past and that could potentially harm us in the future. Most of us probably believe that we "know it (harm) when we see it." We also frequently sense the presence of potential harm and quickly determine when a situation may be dangerous. The fight or flight response which ensues is and has for millennia been key to the survival both of individuals and of our species.

The primary issue in the recognition of harm is a factual one. Are we right or wrong about the occurrence of some harm or about a potential harm? Does it really hurt or not? Occasionally, we work ourselves into such a fearful state of mind that we fail to recognize that something we assumed would be bad or destructive has not hurt, after all. Such decisions are often almost a matter of reflex, and hence fear-governed assessments are difficult to change. Nevertheless, they must sometimes be changed because at least occasionally our initial conclusions will have been incorrect. Consequently, and particularly in important cases, we need to verify whether some harm exists, or does not.

When something appears harmful to us, either potentially or actually, we need to ascertain whether the harm is "real." If the "recipient" of the suspected harm is pretending to have been injured for one reason or another (which is not an uncommon occurrence, for suffering brings us responsive attention and support), then it is hardly the case that some harm is being done. (Small children figure this out quite early.) There are also erroneous or mistaken claims of harm. We occasionally do make mistakes in our own perceptions as, for example, when a poorly sung song could be misconstrued as a cry for help. Furthermore, harm is not usually a matter of objective or standardized pain thresholds: some things that will cause pain to one person will not necessarily have the same effect on another. Generally, however, when pain is being felt, harm is occurring. And while some people have especially low thresholds of pain, if they are in pain, then harm is occurring.

The element of harm must also have some substance; the injury cannot be trivial. Furthermore, because we cannot always tell from an initial set of facts whether an event is or will be harmful, any determination we wish to make may require consideration not only of the act and its immediate consequences but also of its context and its more long-term ramifications. Accidentally brushing against someone's arm is not usually harmful; but if it is perceived as an unwanted sexual advance, it would be. That is to say, what in most circumstances would be an essentially harmless act in and of itself can sometimes become or lead to more significant harm. Whenever the consequence of the act may occur, however, a minimum threshold of negative effect must be exceeded in order to claim that harm has been done and therefore that evil may be present.

Must harm actually occur before we can find that evil (or at least the first element of it) is present, or can it merely be threatened? We usually do not claim that harm is being done *to others* in someone's bad thoughts, particularly when they remain on the level of thought and do not lead to any action. Rather, such harm begins to occur when a person starts implementing an evil plan—when someone actually begins to do something that would be harmful to another (e.g., a conspiracy to commit murder or an attempted murder). In such situations, the threats have become real, and others are justified in engaging in active self-defense. This is particularly true when the attempt or conspiracy becomes known to others, because then the fear that this knowledge brings to the would-be victims is in itself a real harm. (It is also a harm which must be taken into consideration in addition to the harm of the actual injury, if it were subsequently to occur.) Even in the absence of the knowledge of others, however, we may ascribe evil to the slightest act that begins to implement any serious plan aimed at injuring another unjustly.

The identification of actual and not insubstantial harm can be approached in several different ways. Many forms of harm are readily discerned from the physical or mental pain and suffering that they inflict upon us. In the broadest sense of the term, harm is any kind of injury that accompanies some kind of corresponding damage or deprivation. Harm is often (but not necessarily) accompanied by a sensation of pain. A second perspective can be developed by using a frame of reference like Maslow's. Harm occurs when our legitimate needs and wants are not met, and we all have certain kinds of basic and higher needs and wants. Consequently, anything that prevents us from satisfying one or more of those needs or wants would be "harmful"—anything from the deprivation of food or sleep to a loss of security or self-esteem.[1] Harm can also be understood from a third perspective, namely, as a dimension of the "negative ground of being." Thus, if we are moving toward or have arrived at any of the conditions that make up that negative ground, which consists of the bad things in life (like unhappiness or injury or captivity), then we are probably being harmed or have been harmed.

The three frameworks discussed here and in the previous chapter help us recognize the element of harm in what may be an occurrence of evil. While they are not the only ways in which we can identify harm in a given situation, each of them provides a distinct and potentially effective means of determining whether harm has occurred or will occur in any action or in any potential action. Their use can therefore aid us in deciding whether we need to proceed further with an inquiry into evil or immorality. Indeed, this is usually the starting point for such an effort; for if we do not see any harm or potential harm, we rarely suspect that anything evil may have happened or may be happening; and consequently, we tend not to look into it any further. It is usually harm or potential harm that first triggers our suspicions about evil.

Broadly defined, harm occurs frequently. Every one of us is affected by it many times every day. Indeed, on a small scale, harm occurs so often that, of necessity, we must essentially ignore most of

---

1. Of course, "over-satisfaction" of some of these needs or wants can also present problems, for we can be harmed by excesses as well as by deprivations of them.

it, if we are not to be overwhelmed. But more substantial cases of harm or injury occur fairly frequently as well. They vary in degree and duration, but it is simply a fact of life that we sometimes suffer significant harm. It might, however, be added that a considerable amount of the harm that we encounter—at least for most of us, most of the time—is *not* evil and is *not* the result of any evil, since it is often the case that one or both of the other two elements of evil are not present. In other words, if a decision or an action is to have ethical ramifications, both of the other essential elements of evil must be present, as well.

Recognizing the Element of
Responsibility for Causing Harm

Recognizing Causation

Analysis of potential responsibility for a harmful act first requires a look at causation. Whether somebody *caused* something bad to happen to another person or object is, like the question of harm itself, primarily a factual matter: Either they did cause it, or they did not. In order to determine whether something was evil, we must make this second factual determination. And without accurate factual findings on both causation and harm, we are unable to make valid moral judgments about any act that might be evil.

Making a determination about causation will sometimes be the easiest part of an inquiry into evil, but there may also be times when it will be the most difficult. It is, nonetheless, a necessary element in any finding concerning evil; hence, we need to exercise caution in arriving at these conclusions.

Causation is not only a matter of the origins of an action; it is also a matter of clearly identifying consequences and connecting them to the action performed. When we think about "causes" we are usually looking backwards, tracing the effect to the cause. But knowledge of causation is also what helps us look forward with reasoned and often correct expectations. In other words, when we see an event occur, we can frequently predict what effect it will have and what its immediate consequences will be. This forward-looking aspect of causation is perhaps even more important to us than the backward-looking one; the past is finished, and we can only adapt to the future. Understanding causation allows us to accurately anticipate the outcome of events we are now witnessing, and either to prepare for the anticipated consequences or to try to change the "causes" and their potential effects in midstream so as to be more likely to achieve our goals.

We recognize causes and apply our knowledge of them both retroactively and prospectively in two principal ways. We draw on the body of general knowledge that we have about how the world works, and we also make particular investigations into specific phenomena that attract our attention.

Throughout our lifetimes, each of us individually builds a body of knowledge about the world and how it generally works. This knowledge is based upon both formal education and informal learning from experience. Our basic life lessons from childhood provided us with knowledge of routine causes for and the routine consequences of most daily phenomena. For example, pressing the light switch makes the light goes on; and flavoring our food in a certain way makes if taste different and better. Similarly, if the light is on, someone must have pressed the switch; and if the food tastes salty, someone must have salted it. Thus, whenever we see a given effect, we can fairly accurately conclude that the cause which we know generally brings it about did indeed precede it; and conversely, whenever we observe something to be happening which we know to produce a certain effect, we can dependably anticipate the effect that will follow. Our success in navigating through the major part of our daily lives is dependent upon a broad general knowledge of what we might term normal, usual or typical causes and consequences.

The other way we come to recognize causes and consequences is by investigating them directly. In doing so, we expand and render more precise our knowledge. This process involves: (1) framing the question (i.e., selecting a subject and determining whether we are seeking a cause or a consequence); (2) identifying the test(s) we can use to obtain an answer; (3) applying the test; (4) observing the results; and (5) drawing conclusions based upon our observations. We use this process almost instinctively when we are faced with the problem of identifying a particular cause because it has proven to be so useful to us in the past. Consider the following example: (1) We ask "What caused that sound outside?"; then we surmise (2) "If I look out the window I may be able to see something that would help me figure it out"; then we (3) look out the window and state (4) "I see a dog running from an overturned garbage can." Finally, we conclude that (5) "The noise must have been caused by the dog knocking over the can." We may skip over some parts of the process if we have to or if we feel that they are not needed, and we may approximate and guess at various points. It is my contention, however, that while we may not normally think of our discovery of a cause/effect relationship as a process consisting of these discrete steps, we regularly employ them when we are thinking carefully.

If knowing a cause or a consequence is *really* important to us, and if it involves a phenomenon that is susceptible to scientific proof, and if we have the time and resources to devote to it, then we tend either to use or to rely on someone else's use of a special and more refined application of this causation-discovery process—namely, the scientific method. The steps employed in the application of the scientific method are generally: (1) observation; (2) hypothesis; (3) tests of the hypothesis (through controlled experiments); (4) conclusions based upon the tests; and (5) replications by others. Causes and consequences that have been identified by the application of the scientific method are commonly thought to be among the most reliable that we have. We therefore usually give greater credence to claims about causes and consequences discovered and confirmed through applications of scientific method than to those which may have been acquired in some other manner.

A large part of any effort to identify causes and consequences, whether the scientific or the more informal discovery process is being utilized, is trying to disprove some of our initial guesses or hypotheses. Often we can eliminate several of the likely candidates for causes or consequences; and the more of them we can accurately eliminate, the more likely we will be able to identify correctly the actual cause or consequence from among the smaller pool of remaining possibilities. This process of elimination is sometimes referred to as "falsification": we figure out how to disprove something (if indeed it is false), and then proceed to show that the disproof that we have developed is valid. If we find a disproof, then our search for the true cause of a known effect is advanced.

Our efforts at identifying causes are more successful when we understand that there are problems that can routinely lead us astray, and then watch out for them. Some of these have long been well-known, such as temporal coincidence without any (obvious) connection between cause and effect, multiple (and possibly simultaneous) causation for a single effect, intentional deceptions (usually concerning agency), and so forth. It is easy to overlook some causes, and sometimes we will really want to avoid finding certain things to be causes and thus ignore the evidence supporting them. However, being aware of and alert for these routine types of obstacles should help us apply the process more accurately.

To draw a conclusion, we have to collect the relevant information and see whether it confirms or disconfirms our hypothesis. If it disconfirms it, we then have to try to figure out what the data might confirm alternatively. We make inferences from the information available to us, and we also rely on the general body of knowledge we have about how the world works. If a preliminary conclusion about the existence of a cause is consistent with our general understanding about the way the world works, we find that the existence of the cause we have been seeking is further confirmed. If, on the other hand, a conclusion we have drawn diverges from our general knowledge about the world, we may feel suspicious about the accuracy of our finding and thus need to go back and review, or even restart, the confirmation process. Finally, we can improve the accuracy of our conclusions by seeking out the observations and opinions of others who have considerable knowledge about the specific phenomenon or type of phenomenon in question. That is, we can appeal to external authorities for additional confirmation or refutation of our tentative conclusions about a certain cause or causes.

When can we rely on our conclusions about causation? Where moral judgments are involved, and particularly those which carry with them potentially damaging consequences, we should probably try to mirror the standard that has been set in the legal world for determining causation in most civil lawsuits and not be satisfied with anything less than a conclusion that is based upon a "preponderance of the evidence."

Recognizing the Capacity to
Avoid Causing the Harm

Once we have found that a person has actually caused real harm, we still have some other issues to consider before we can properly attribute responsibility (and also, potentially, culpability) to them. The first of these is whether the agent either knew or should have known that harm would result from his or her actions—a determination which cannot be made until we are certain that the agent has sufficient mental capacity to be cognizant of that.

It is not the case that all of us have the foundational level of understanding necessary for making accurate assessments of our world, nor do we all possess the ability to reason from those assessments. These problems may be permanent (e.g., in cases of a severe brain injury or other mental disability), or they may be temporary (e.g., a fleeting mental disorientation). Severe mental retardation would, at least in many situations, mean that an individual should not be held responsible for some of his or her actions because he or she was not capable of having any effective foreknowledge of the consequences. If Joe does not know that dropping a heavy bag on someone would have harmful consequences for that person, then we cannot hold Joe morally responsible for doing so.

Usually we do not need to spend much time making an assessment about mental retardation or about a disabling mental illness, for these are often relatively obvious conditions. The issue immediately presents itself to us when such a problem is present; and when it does not, we usually do not pause to consider it. Unless and until a specific question about responsibility is raised by some subsequent event (e.g., an unusual action by the agent or information supplied by someone else about the agent's mental capacity), we generally move ahead to thinking about other issues in our analysis.

Making a determination about a claim of temporary inability to know that harmful consequences might follow from a given action can be more difficult. Such a consideration can, nevertheless, be important to determining whether to hold someone responsible for harm caused when he or she arguably was not in a condition to know about it. Consider the example of a person who, while coming out of anesthesia following surgery, does or says something hurtful or injurious to another. This issue is further complicated when the disorientation that caused the temporary inability to reason well was self-induced (e.g., through the consumption of alcohol or other mind-affecting chemicals).

Whether someone who has a basic mental competency has (or had) foreknowledge of some particular potential harm, or whether that person knows (or knew) that some harm could result from a specific action, is a fact that we try to determine using the same methods we use to discover what others know (or knew) about any other facts. First, we listen to what the agent says. If before or after the action occurs, a person says something like, "I know this is going to hurt you" or "I was afraid that would happen," such a remark constitutes a direct admission of that knowledge. Other things people say can also lead us to the same conclusion, albeit indirectly, through such statements as "Oh, no! Not again!" Furthermore, we sometimes infer from people's actions that they were knowledgeable of the potential consequences. If someone does not appear to be surprised by a dramatic outcome, for instance, it suggests that they knew or suspected what was coming all along. However, while it may sometimes be relatively easy to determine whether someone knew before they took an action that it could have a harmful consequence, in other cases we may just have to look harder at their verbal and nonverbal behavior and make the most reasonable and best supported inferences possible under the circumstances.

Even when it is impossible to determine that someone actually knew of the likely harmful consequence of an act before it was done, there is still the question of whether the agent should have known about it. This would, of course, constitute a more subjective conclusion. However, in the absence of a fairly substantiated determination about an agent's anticipating that his action would result in a harmful consequence, we need to look at this other type of responsibility for advance knowledge of that consequence. Even if someone did not know that harm would follow from a specific action, if he should have known about it, then he can be held responsible for it.

This is possible because we recognize that a certain level of basic knowledge about how the world works is fairly equally distributed among people. Thus, even if we do not know about a specific potential consequence, if it is the type of thing that most thinking people would recognize as a possible outcome of the situation, then we may determine that responsibility needs to be assigned for causing the harm. One reason we do this is because it makes sense, but another is because the world works much better if we hold people responsible for exercising at least a basic level of carefulness with regard to their actions. If we did not do this, we would have to contend with considerably more harmful actions.

Attempting to determine what someone should have known in any specific situation requires us to consider the availability and distribution of the relevant knowledge. If a significant number of people believe that in contemplating an action they would have become aware that it might have harmful consequences, then it would be fair to conclude that the agent who actually inflicted the harm should have realized this, too. In other words, "should have knowns" are established mainly by reflective consensus.

Only when we conclude that someone who took what turned out to be an action with a harmful consequence really did not know and was not obligated to know that such a consequence could have come from that act would we be correct in concluding that he or she was not responsible for it. When someone takes an action that causes a harm and knew or should have known that the harm was possible, however, we will usually consider him or her to be responsible for causing it.

Knowledge of a potential outcome may be the primary part of our analysis here, but there is yet another factor which requires our attention, namely the issue of self-control. In order to hold people responsible for potentially harmful actions, we have to determine not only that they were generally capable of controlling themselves so that they could have avoided such actions, but also that they could actually have avoided performing the particular actions in question.

In general, self-control has both physical and mental aspects. Due to illness or injury, some people are physically unable to control all of their actions (e.g., victims of Parkinson's disease). Other people do not have the mental ability to control their physical actions, and hence would not always be responsible for them.

In cases in which general self-control is not an issue, we normally act of our own volition. That is, for each action we perform, it is the case that we might have done something else, or we might have done nothing at all. On rare occasions, however, we may have only one option for action in the face of certain physical constraints or coercive factors or agents; and when it can be said that we really could not have avoided engaging in the action, then we should not be held responsible for the act or for the harm resulting from it.

It is sometimes argued that culpability should only attach to harm that was intentionally caused, i.e., when the choice to do the harmful act was unforced and when the person inflicting the harm both understood the significance of his actions and evaluated the choice ahead of time (which may be referred to as an "autonomous" action).[2] When these conditions are not met, and a nonautonomous action causes harm, the agent who caused it would arguably not be culpable. The problem with this argument, in my opinion, is that it excuses far too many morally wrong acts solely on the ground that doing what is right may be difficult. The fact is, however, that many things that some people may call "nonautonomous" and thus consider to be "excusable" (because of having had a domineering father or because of a need to focus on company profits) are really not beyond our control, if we are willing to make a strong effort to overcome the influences that impel us toward immoral actions: people free themselves from such limiting conditions, just as they overcome vices that lead to evil. The truly "nonautonomous" action is quite rare, and its exculpation should apply only to those who, like infants and some of the severely mentally ill, really have no effective or potentially effective control over their actions. The extent to which other excuses for causing harm might legitimately be considered are more comprehensively and appropriately taken up when we ascribe degrees of immorality to actions for which we have been responsible,[3] and not when we first determine whether someone is or is not responsible for causing some harm.

---

2. *See, e.g.,* John Kekes, "The Reflexivity of Evil," 15 *Soc. Pol. Phil.* (Winter, 1998), pp. 216-232.
3. See Chapter 5.

In an important case, the agent's capacity to avoid causing the harm should usually be adjudicated, wherever possible, by consensus after due deliberation on the basis of all of the available facts. If, after doing this, we find the act could have been avoided by someone who knew or should have known of the harm that his or her action could cause, we should (in most cases) consider him or her to be responsible for it, and hence also to be culpable for it.

Recognizing the Element of
the Lack of Justification for the Harm

The Nature of the Means/Ends Defense

People who are responsible for causing undeserved harm are often—perhaps most often—considered to be culpable for them. However, such a person may occasionally escape culpability when we consider the harmful act in a situation in which the harm to one person may be justified by a benefit that somehow also results from that same action—a benefit either to the victim or to others. This defense against culpability is proffered far too often; but in certain situations, most of us would find no culpability in the agent inflicting the harm because of the "good" that ultimately came from it. The gist of this argument is that even though the harmful action, when viewed in isolation, may have been undeserved by its victim, it was nevertheless actually justified for some other reason. Consequently, when seen in a larger context, it cannot be said to be morally wrong or really evil.

All kinds of "reasons" are suggested for this purpose; and while many of them are obviously specious, a number of others are frequently accepted as adequate justifications for actions which, but for those justifications, would be considered morally wrong. When we try to justify the harm that we are causing by reference to a "higher" good or purpose, and thus try to enlarge the context in which the "evil act" should be morally understood and judged, we are making a means/ends argument: We are attempting to justify the "evil" of the specific harmful act under consideration, and we are, in essence, attempting to nullify its evil because of the higher good to which the act might lead (or might have led).

Our world and our lives consist of a succession of cause and effect events, which, when described in functional terms, often are successive means and ends. "Ends" in this sense are things we want to obtain or accomplish. What we can prepare for breakfast today (nourishment being an end in this context) was defined in part by what we purchased at the grocery store yesterday (the items of food being a means in this context). If we make a widget today, then it can serve as a means for us to obtain money which we can then use to purchase other things and hence to achieve other ends (e.g., through the acquisition of something else that we need or want), which we will use in order to accomplish something else (e.g., to keep us warm or to make us look attractive), and so on. In short, life involves cycles of causation. When we get what we need or want, we not only achieve a fulfillment and satisfaction in that accomplishment in and of itself, but at some point we often also use that which we have gained as another means for doing or attaining other things. In one context or another and from one perspective or another, just about everything that occurs can be seen as but a temporary "end"—one thing is, when gained, often already on its way to being used as a means to facilitate the coming into being of something else; and conversely, everything that comes into being as an "end" does so though prior means—things that were, at one time and in some sense, ends in themselves.

This interrelation between means and ends is central to our moral lives. While some tend to think of the term "means/ends" only in a pejorative sense and as ethically invalid because of the many problems people cause in trying to justify bad means through highly questionable "good ends," we apply means/ends analyses throughout our moral lives (and not just when we consider "bad" means). We do not usually recognize this fact, but whenever we do one thing in order to accomplish something else that is either good or bad, we are using a means to obtain some end. Using good means to achieve good ends and using either good or bad means to obtain bad ends do not present us with any moral dilemmas: The former is always good and accepted, and the latter are always bad and condemned. Bad-means-to-good-ends arguments, on the other hand, do give us problems; and they not only abound, but they also can and do confuse us.

Most of the time when we employ a means/ends defense in response to a charge of having caused some undeserved harm, the situation is one in which we have *intended* to engage in the harmful action. We *know* that we are likely to cause harm or that we have already caused it, but we believe we *should* cause or *should have* caused that harm because of a greater good that will come from it in some way. In other words, when we look at the third element in our analysis of evil and ask whether the harmful action which was done was justified or not, if we find that the act and the ensuing harm were both intended, we will often hear (if we are listening) a means/ends argument attempting to justify it. And, given that this type of argument can be quite powerful, we will frequently be confronted with such a "defense" even when the evildoer knows that it is absolutely spurious. Convincing others that the harm that he is causing is or may be acceptable helps him achieve his goals; and even if he is not successful in convincing them of its ethical acceptability, his arguments might at least cause confusion and thereby render them incapable of action. While we may also occasionally use a means/ends argument in a case in which we would be deemed culpable even though our action was unintentional, we would likely do so only in retrospect, or as an afterthought. In other words, when we are intent upon acting for a higher purpose, we generally have that purpose in mind at the time we act.

A means/ends argument claims that while I intend to do something that may cause a "smaller" harm through this means now, my overall intent in the larger context is to do good in the longer term, and not only to do good but also to do a "higher" good that outweighs the good of avoiding this currently harmful act. Culpability is avoided insofar as, viewed in the larger context, my intention is to do good, and I really am doing it—and not just harm. Unfortunately, because of the complexity (and perhaps in some sense, the perversity) of this world, in order to do that higher good, I simply have to do this lower bad.

A means/ends argument therefore states that we are intending to do some larger good in the long run and takes the position that this fact justifies our doing this smaller bad thing in the present—it is a necessary step we must take toward reaching some higher goal. The victim of our actions simply happens to be in the way of our achieving this higher good—either by some accident of time and place or by the design of someone else. To use this argument, however, we have to be willing to risk employing what are at least some morally problematic means in our effort to reach an objective which should, in our mind, have ethical priority. Furthermore, we have to be willing to claim that what may appear to be immoral when we are focusing only on the act that constitutes the means will become morally acceptable when we refocus on the larger frame of reference that includes the end(s).

Another view of the means/ends argument suggests that the end need not be conceived of as a positive accomplishment, but may also be viewed as the avoidance of a negative outcome. From this perspective, a means that would be considered "wrong" in and of itself could nevertheless be justified in cases in which the evil that would result if the end were not achieved would outweigh the wrong that was caused by the means. In other words, if the end, stated in positive terms, was to save the life of a child, and the "wrongful" means needed to accomplish this benevolent action was to tell a lie to someone else (thereby ignoring an obligation to fidelity), considering the situation from the perspective of aiming for a positive outcome, we would say that the higher good (saving an innocent life) outweighs the wrong of telling a lie. Considering this example from the perspective of avoiding a negative outcome, however, we would say that the evil which attaches to failure to perform the benevolent duty of saving an innocent life far outweighs the evil of telling the lie that is necessary in order to do so. "Avoiding the greater evil" could then become the relevant principle to be applied to at least some means/ends discussions. Just as we necessarily weigh and compare goods (e.g., whether we should give $5 or $10 to today's charity), so we also weigh and balance evils. We apply means/ends analyses to comparative evils as well as to comparative goods. Consequently, if the only way to avoid a great evil is by doing a lesser evil, or if the failure to achieve some end would be a bigger wrong than the wrong that would come from employing the means, we should consider the means to be morally justified. It would then be considered morally acceptable to do a lesser evil if that were the only way to avoid a much greater one.

The basic premise of means/ends arguments is therefore that an immoral act (in some smaller context) can lead to a moral good (in the larger context). In other words, we are asserting here that it is not only the case that bad can lead to good, but also that bad can become an acceptable part of a process which aims toward the good—not only that a wrong can lead to a right, but also that it is sometimes the "right thing" to do, and that it may even be morally necessary (i.e., a "necessary evil"). Stated in such direct terms, these claims surprise and almost astound. How can we possibly justify doing bad things in a moral world?[4]

The answer to this question is twofold: "Because the moral world is a complex place," and "Because we successfully use, and we should use, means/ends arguments in making ethical decisions all the time." Making ethical decisions really *is* a matter of focus: if we narrow our focus too much, we will lose an entire forest for a single tree. We have to try to keep in mind all of the potential intended and unintended ramifications of our moral choices; and we need to place all of our moral decisions in their proper larger contexts, lest we cause greater harm by our ethical shortsightedness or narrow provincialism. It is always incumbent upon us to fulfill moral duties in a larger context. In cases in which some moral decision is immediately necessary, we may sometimes overlook some of our "larger context" duties; but if we only focus on each act singly, we will, at least occasionally, breach significantly larger moral duties. Those who would argue that the flight crew should not use violent means to subdue a terrorist hijacker (if that were the only way to do so) because we should not hurt others (including those who may be standing near to the hijacker) are ignoring the crew's continuing benevolence duties to the other passengers, which specifically require the crew to prevent grave undeserved harm from coming to those passengers when it is within their power to do so. A metamorphosis of a harmful means actually can occur, and, conversely, a good end can emerge from a bad means, just as a butterfly emerges from a caterpillar.

---

4. Particularly in a world in which the aphorism, "Two wrongs do not make a right," has such credence.

I believe that all of us accept and use means/ends arguments, even if we do not like the idea of them, even if we claim that we reject them, even if we vehemently argue that no one should ever accept them, even if we regularly cite the maxim that "The ends do not justify the means," and even if we are initially repulsed by the suggestion that they are or should be acceptable. In support of this conclusion, I offer the following propositions:

a. It is morally acceptable to chastise one person in public in order to give others pause before they would repeat the observed mistake, even if a private reprimand would have been sufficient punishment for the wrongdoer;

b. It is acceptable to shove one bystander into another in order to prevent the second one from falling on the subway tracks in front of an oncoming train;

c. It is ethical for a pharmaceutical company to charge high prices for medicines which are necessary to basic health today in order to generate sufficient funds for developing drugs that would help others in the future;

d. It is morally acceptable to encourage others to go on a hunger strike or otherwise to cause themselves some physical harm in order to end an injustice;

e. It is morally acceptable for a government to condemn private property for purposes of building a public road;

f. It is morally acceptable for a country to require young men to fight wars to advance the interests of that country;

g. It is acceptable for legislators sometimes to compromise on some of their political positions and principles and vote for bills that contain some things that they believe to be bad if they conclude that the bills contain, on balance, more good features than bad;

h. It would have been ethical for someone to have assassinated Hitler in the early 1930's in order to have prevented the Holocaust;

j. It is ethically acceptable to risk killing a limited number of noncombatants in time of war in order to destroy an important military target;

k. It is moral to require all persons to be vaccinated against a deadly and fast-spreading plague, even if some people do not want it and even if some of them would die from negative reactions to the vaccine;

l. It is ethical for a policeman in hot pursuit of a murderer to appropriate a private citizen's car if it is needed for the chase and apprehension;

m. It is morally acceptable for rescue workers to storm through one person's apartment to reach someone else on a ledge and try to prevent him from jumping;

n. It would be acceptable for a father to promise his young children any treat to inspire them to leave a burning house, even if he knew that he could not fulfill that promise[5]; and

o. God gave His only Son to redeem the sins of the world.

If you agreed with *any* of the above assertions (or if for some specific reason or reasons you did not, but you know that there is a similar assertion with which you would agree), then you accept the basic rationale of means/ends arguments, and you accept their status as a paradigm for one of the primary defenses that we can make in response to charges of immorality whenever undeserved harm has been caused to others. The paradigm not only works in routine moral decision-making, but also for the larger moral issues of every day. A

---

5. See the Lotus Suttra on skillful means and useful lies.

means/ends argument is simply an ethical tool that we must employ if we are interested in living ethical lives. People who deny its validity may claim that they find moral purity by temporarily dwelling in a sort of artificial vacuum, but they soon encounter contradictions and conflicts that cause them to flounder. For example, if you do not tell a lie that could have saved a child's life, then you are at least indirectly responsible for the child's death, and you have breached your duty of benevolence toward that child; and having done this would place you in a horrible moral position—you would have done evil by omission in the larger context because you chose to do only a relatively lesser good (truth-telling) in a smaller one.[6]

But while means/ends arguments *can* work, they do *not* always work. Hannah Arendt thought that means/ends arguments should never be employed because they would inevitably be misused, and that condoning any use of them at all would lead to even more evils.[7] But it can be argued that everything has potential for mis-use—especially powerful ethical tools, like laws. Anyone who agrees with Immanuel Kant's claim that the correct test for the ethicalness (or unethicalness) of an action is its universalizability ("Act only on a maxim which you agree should be a universal law") could not simultaneously accept the means/ends paradigm as a logical instrument for evaluating moral decisions. If a perfect hierarchy of ethical values existed and could be applied in every situation, then perhaps this text would apply. But such a hierarchy has not been discovered—and may not be discoverable[8]; so as circumstances require, we employ means/ends arguments to help us resolve many of our ethical dilemmas.

To all of this, however, I would add the following caveat: we must be exceedingly careful when, in an effort to achieve some right end, we permit ourselves to engage in an action that is wrong, even in a limited context. If it proves to be the case that we are in error,

---

6. It is in the larger context that this type of argument is sometimes called the "greater-good defense."
7. "Personal Responsibility Under Dictatorship," *The Listener* 72 (August 6, 1964), pp. 185-187, 205.
8. See, for example, *Being Ethical*, pp. 52-55.

we will, at the least, have done one unredeemed wrong, and our actions could end up promoting more immorality than we were trying to bargain against in the first place. Nevertheless, using means/ends tests is absolutely necessary in any effort to adjudicate these issues fairly, for we must take into consideration the broader perspectives and larger contexts in which we live.

The Lack of Justification from the Perspective of the Victim

Harm done by a person or persons to a victim is unjust if no valid moral reason exists for it to have happened. From the perspective of the victim, harm would be justifiable if it were a matter of: deserved punishment, legitimate self-defense, appropriate instruction, or any other circumstances in which the harmful means are, relative to the person suffering the initial harm, outweighed by some direct benefit to that person.

The first of the issues here derives from the fact that, at least some of the time, the harm that we receive is precisely what we deserve. Doing harm is not necessarily immoral, and therefore the conscious infliction of harm will not always be wrong, but rather sometimes will be deserved.

Undeservedness, which includes everything that is not "deserved," is simply one facet of the issue of unjustness. Undeservedness may cause us to construe the object of the harm as a "victim"—at least in the context of that act alone. Deservedness, on the other hand, is a characteristic of justly inflicted harm. In other words, if the harm was clearly deserved, the action will escape further suspicion of and examination for immorality.

To determine what is undeserved, we must first understand what "deserved harm" is. Such harm must occur as a response to something that was previously done (or should have been done but was not) by the present recipient of that harm. Harm may be deserved as punishment if a person has previously committed an act for which he or she is culpable and for which harm is merited (e.g., if he has struck someone else without provocation). Deserved harm may also be inflicted on another in an instance of legitimate self-defense (e.g., while wrestling with an aggressor in an attempt to keep from being clubbed without good reason).

To determine deservedness relative to these two issues (punishment and self-defense), we need to understand and ethically analyze the prior actions of the recipient of the present harm. For both of these issues, deservedness requires that we morally judge the earlier actions of the person who has been, is now being, or is about to be, harmed. When we have ascertained the relevant facts as best we can, we must to place a moral value on them. Were those prior actions on the part of the recipient of the current harm (or potential harm) morally culpable in such a way as to justify a response either of punishment or of potentially harmful self-defense? "Deserved harm" is simply one type of justice meted out in a given context; it is a merited detrimental action toward or injury to its recipient.

In order to become adept at discerning when a harmful response is justified, we need to begin with a basic understanding of justice. The subject of justice is, like so many related topics, one that fills volumes and has preoccupied wise people for whole lifetimes. A good starting point for a working understanding of it can be gleaned from *A Theory of Justice*, by John Rawls, in which he suggested that we can determine what is just in a given situation by resolving the problem in such a way that the solution would seem fair to us regardless of which role we happened to occupy.[9] This exercise requires a certain degree of imagination and empathy, but it provides us with an excellent guideline for determining whether justice has been done in particular cases. We have all been victims of an unjust action (at least in small ways) from time to time; and most of us have also caused unjustified harm to others (at least in small ways) from time to time. In cases in which one person has clearly done something wrong to another, it is helpful to place ourselves in the positions of both the victim and the perpetrator when attempting to determine what sort of response, if any, would be justified. If I identify with the victim, would it be fair for me (or someone else) to punish the wrongdoer? And if so, how, and how much? But that matter does not end with a reprisal based solely on the victim's

---

9. Harvard University Press (1971). (See also the Golden Rule and its various formulations and corollaries.)

perspective. I should also try to identify with the wrongdoer and ask, if *I* had done this wrong, what should I reasonably expect as a fair response from an innocent victim? What sort of punishment and how much of it, if any, would *then* seem to be appropriate?

One of the ways in which we can try to establish such things is by attempting to ascertain each person's "due." Generally speaking, everyone is owed at least minimally moral behavior from everyone else because of our rudimentary duties of benevolence toward each other. We should neither cause harm to others nor do injustice to them. But this is also to be understood reciprocally. Everyone is due justice from everyone else, so we are all entitled to receive our "due" from others, as well.

Justice would provide us with positive rewards for the good things that we have done or achieved, both individually and collectively. For example, wages are paid in exchange for labor, and a fair share of resources and opportunities is owed to us within the groups to which we belong. However, those with whom we have special role relationships—our families, for example, are "due" more from us than are strangers. Our duty of fidelity to them expands our general duty of benevolence to those with whom we share such relationships. But in this connection we also need to note that even though our highest benevolent duty is that of being charitable—of giving people more than would otherwise be their "due," not everyone is owed acts of charity from us. If we were so excessively generous, we would quickly deplete our own resources and perhaps even become needy ourselves, which is not a positive moral development. That is to say, our individual capacity for charity is infinitesimal in comparison with the needs of others.

Arguably, justice would also deliver negative consequences for the bad things we have done, in which case some punishment would be "due" for every moral transgression. In a moral world, bad actions deserve bad consequences of some sort, not only for purposes of retribution, but also as part of an effort to deter or prevent similar future acts. Of course, many—if not most—moral transgressions remain unpunished (at least, in this lifetime). Too many bad things happen; and we would have neither the time nor the energy to deal with all of the wrongs that occur, even if we were to know about them. It is hard enough to handle our own personal moral lives even moderately well, let alone devote a great deal of time to those of others. Nevertheless, people who are interested in trying to make the world a more moral place must, from time to time, become involved in efforts to punish moral transgressions.

The other major deservedness issue involves self-defense. For purposes of self-defense, we are entitled to react individually or corporately not only to keep undeserved harm away from ourselves personally but also in order to prevent others from suffering from a violation of their basic rights. If someone does not intervene to stop aggressors, they cause additional harm which we might have prevented had we acted sooner. Thus, if we are to act out of benevolence, we must at times cause some harm to wrongdoers in defense not only of ourselves but also of others. Indeed, it is often only by such a response that we can stop a wrongdoer in the act of attempting to inflict harm as well as deter other potential wrongdoers who may be observing the proceedings.

Who can and who should decide issues of deservedness in these situations? As a practical matter and at least to some extent, we all should—and indeed, must—do so, both individually and collectively. Moral life is a social enterprise, and our actions are all integral to it. When we are directly exposed to what we suspect to be some evil, we should first try to determine for ourselves the moral "dues" owed by the various participants in the situation by applying the guidelines that we use for these purposes. To do so effectively, we will often need to ascertain whether any special role relationship exists that might require an adjustment to our usual benevolence obligations. If the one taking an action was a relative of the victim, for example, harm caused by defense of the victim or punishment imposed in response to the harm may be appropriately undertaken by that relative even if that might not be the case had the victim been a stranger. A child who fails to defend a younger sibling from harassment by another child, for instance, may be held culpable when that would not necessarily have been the case if he or she failed to do the same thing for a stranger (although the particular circumstances would, of course, have to be closely examined). We can therefore conclude that where a special or primary relationship is involved, loyalty duties may strongly influence whether and the extent to which a response of self-defense or punishment is morally appropriate. If we determine that no such relationship exists, then our moral response will be dictated by the general guidelines governing punishment and self-defense.

Once we have worked out for ourselves what we believe is deserved, then, if we have time and the opportunity to do so, we should try to learn how others—especially those with moral authority and expertise—would evaluate the situation. This aids us in making judgments that are balanced. In addition, while those who are involved in doing and receiving harm and those closely related to them are necessarily concerned with these decisions, our larger social groups and institutions should also become engaged in the process. We have socially established norms and standard punishments as a result of our collective experience with all kinds of evils; and absent some major social failure, our collectively considered judgment is usually the best means available for determining both deservedness of punishment and the appropriateness of certain responses to threatened or inflicted harms.

Who can and should actually impose a deserved punishment? For purposes of social efficiency and convenience, we have created certain formal roles for the persons who are to perform these functions (such as policemen, judges and jailers). These people fix certain forms of penalties for specific offenses, and we collectively delegate to them a large portion of the work of imposing punishment on wrongdoers. However, there are cases in which the victim or intended victim is justified in meting out punishment directly, particularly where self-defense has become necessary or in cases in which an infraction is relatively insignificant. The several variables involved in determining who can legitimately impose deserved harm or who may intervene in defense of an intended victim include: (1) the egregiousness of the injury or potential harm; (2) the degree of culpability which can be assigned to the perpetrator for the harm; (3) whether or not a special relationship is involved; and (4) the opportunity to have an impact. However, I would add that it is extremely important that deserved punishment be meted out and that defenses be made by the right persons or groups. If it is handled by the wrong persons or groups, harm that would have been deserved if it had come from an appropriate person or group can either initiate or perpetuate a cycle of unjustified harms.

In addition to that harm which is deserved because of some wrong previously done, harm may also not be unjust if it is employed as a legitimate form of instruction. In attempting to adjudicate the justness of a harm in the context of instruction, we need a good understanding of both the situation and the "student." Some instruction is necessary for self-preservation. Small children must learn not to play with fire even if they may feel hurt by the scoldings or punishments to which they are subjected when they persist in doing so. At other times, inflicting "harm" for purposes of instruction may be justified for other reasons. We educate our young not only on matters of self-preservation, but also on those of morality. We owe young people this; it is their due. And when that instruction has to include some hurt or injury in response to an ignorant or immature action on the part of the child (who needs to know and do better), then it is still the child's due and a legitimate end in order for the child to grow correctly. In other words, we have to cultivate our children properly in order for them to have a chance to lead moral lives, and sometimes doing this requires inflicting some type of "harm" as part of that teaching process (even though that harm should be as benign as possible under the circumstances). The primary test of the legitimacy of the imposition of harm in this context is whether the result advances the "student" in some appropriate way. Is the harm that is caused as part of the instruction outweighed by the direct benefit attained? Does it have as a consequence the learner's gaining, for example, a better chance of survival, or becoming self-realized, or being properly loyal?

When harm is justified for purposes of instruction, people who occupy positions of authority relative to the "student" (e.g., parents, teachers, and older siblings) have the primary authority and moral responsibility to determine and undertake such actions as may be appropriate. Parents and caretakers of young children have to enforce "no hitting" rules, for example, until good habits become ingrained, even if that can only be accomplished through some action that the child will clearly perceive as harmful. But legitimate instruction is not limited to children; when any one of us does not understand a risk or is not clear on the appropriate moral action to be taken in a specific situation, we may still need to learn these things through a process that we may find to be painful (e.g., when pulled over for a traffic infraction, we may not only lose time and money, but we may also suffer the embarrassment of a lecture on the dangers of our manner of driving and on our moral responsibility to observe the law).

Finally from the perspective of the victim, the infliction of harm may not be unjust if it will lead to—or be a necessary part of a process that leads to—some other greater benefit for the "victim" himself or herself. If the harm inflicted is small relative to the benefit that the "victim" will receive, and if the benefit is something the "victim" either wants or should have, then the imposition of that harm may not be wrong, and therefore not a part of evil.

Means/ends arguments are thus not limited to situations involving third parties. They are also used when only the "victim" is taken into consideration, and usually in the broader context of the larger, overall impact that something may have on us over a long period of time. In trying to determine whether something is, on balance, right or wrong when it brings both harm and benefit to the same person, divergent ethical considerations often come into play. The pain of a successful surgery, for example, which is an immediate negative on the pleasure/pain/restraint approach to ethics, is outweighed in the longer term by the benefit of a return to health—a positive not only from the longer pain-avoidance perspective, but also in terms of self-realization. We are employing a means/ends argument when we propose that someone would benefit in the long run and possibly obtain some greater good or outcome as a result of a process that involves some short term pain, injury or deprivation.

This type of analysis also challenges, to some degree, our initial conclusion about the real existence of the element of "harm" itself; because if we extend the time frame under consideration, we can sometimes project that there will be some greater good which will more than outweigh the initial harm to the victim. In such cases, the "net" effect on the person receiving the harm will be predominantly positive rather than negative. If we assert that, "This harm which I am proposing to do is not unjust because it is for the 'victim's' own greater good, in the long run," then we are arguing that evil is not occurring because it is not unjust as to the "victim" or because there essentially is insufficient harm (or injury), or both.

Recognizing when this kind of means/ends justification is valid is sometimes easy (as with a medical procedure that hurts but cures), but it can also be very difficult. It is most problematic when the "victim" either has no voice in the decision-making process or is opposed to it because he does not agree that the result would be of greater benefit to him.

In summary, there are at least four different ways in which we may legitimately justify doing harm to another when we consider only the "victim" of that harm. The first two occur when the harm is deserved, as in the case of (a) punishment for a past wrong, or (b) the infliction of harm on another in the process of defending ourselves against an unjust attack. In both of these cases, we cause harm to someone because he or she has caused (or is trying to cause) unjust harm to ourselves or someone else. The third occurs (c) when harming another is part of a process of legitimate instruction that is necessary for the recipient's own well-being or moral development. The fourth manner in which we may justify it is (d) when the harm is part of a process that is the only means of attaining some different but much greater benefit for that person.

Making a moral judgment about the justice or injustice which attaches to some harm done to a victim from the perspective of that person is of critical importance to our recognizing evil and other forms of immorality, because at least some harm *should* come to us in this life in the form of punishment or corrective action, given the way the majority of us seem to live it. Justified harm cannot be regarded as evil. If, however, the harm is not deserved or otherwise justified relative to the one now being harmed, then the third element of evil is probably present.

The Lack of Justification in the Larger Context

Even when we have concluded that harm done to a victim was neither deserved nor justified based on a judgment we have made about a previous action in which he or she might have engaged or some need or condition involving him or her which might have been present, we may still have to consider the morality of the situation within a broader frame of reference before drawing a final conclusion about whether or not any unjustness or evil might attach to it. At this point our attention must refocus on deciding on acceptable (or unacceptable) parameters of means/ends arguments. In some situations, we are aiming to benefit people other than the victim(s)—sometimes only for our own personal benefit, but other times in conjunction with advancing what we deem to be important principles (other than "We should avoid causing harm to innocent people at all costs"). Consequently, we may need to examine more closely the most difficult and problematic types of means/ends arguments, namely those that are made when someone wants so badly to accomplish some major end that he thinks that it is acceptable to do some lesser degree of harm to someone else in the process of attempting to achieve that aim.

Because of the dangers inherent in employing means/ends arguments in which only someone other than the immediate victim benefits, my review of these arguments will begin with some caveats. It is imperative that we be exceedingly careful in thinking through our attempts to justify harmful acts toward others using means/ends arguments. We also need to remember that *almost every* intentional harmdoer will, at one time or another, try to justify his behavior by relying on arguments of this type. It is as if a "means/ends shuffle" has been choreographed into the dance of every agent of intentional harm; for when they are confronted with the wrong entailed in the immediate harm they intend to do, they generally attempt to co-opt the moral playing field by trying to convince themselves and others of the rightness of their intended harms in the context of a larger picture. Very few of the bad actions which have been intentionally carried out in this world have not, according to their perpetrators, been "justified," as they have been accompanied by some means/ends "cover"—albeit one which may prove to have been made of the sheerest of materials. Indeed, the most consummate evildoers have usually become quite adept at offering means/ends arguments which may sound plausible to many but which can, upon closer examination, be shown to be invalid.

We are all capable of being deluded by such means/ends arguments. Even when they are specious, they can serve as effective tools in recruiting people to a cause. Calling people to rally for some seemingly noble end can generate considerable enthusiasm, but such efforts have also led to innumerable individual wrongs along the way—some of which would hardly have seemed justifiable if it had not been for the emotional fervor of the moment in which they were carried out. I suspect that even the most cautious and skeptical of persons have been deceived by means/ends arguments from time to time. We are particularly susceptible to such delusions and forms of coercion when we are already sympathetic toward an overall objective which appears to justify an immediate harm. Hence, we cannot abandon the sound moral judgment necessary to determining whether or not some "greater good" can indeed justify the actions we may be contemplating. The failure to be cautious in such circumstances can, as a consequence, make us parties to great evil. Massacres and genocides, for example, are most often perpetrated by people who rely on means/ends arguments run amuck, which generally have been put as follows: "We are good; they are evil and they are trying to harm us; we must kill all of them to protect ourselves and thereby also make the world a better place." Deceptive means/ends arguments work when they are advanced on a large scale because we are always susceptible to being misled on that level.[10]

Generally speaking, whenever we consider using a potentially dangerous tool or instrument of any kind, we need to understand the risks involved in doing so and know how to diminish them. We can minimize the risks involved in using a means/ends test by becoming familiar with its operating principles and by recognizing some of the main types of errors that we make when we employ this test.

Our applications of means/ends tests can fail in a variety of ways. First, we can be mistaken about the character of the harm which might ensue, about its possible impact, or even about whom it is likely to affect. We can also be wrong about whether the means we have chosen is a necessary step on the way to the end(s) for which we are striving. Furthermore, we can err in assessing the value of the "end" that we are supposedly seeking, and we can make

---

10. Indeed, sometimes it seems that the larger the scale, the easier the deception (perhaps because many of those being deceived tend to relax, relying on others to be morally vigilant and to have carefully considered the matter).

mistakes in balancing the end(s) against the means. But, in addition to the errors we can make in the assessment of contemplated means and ends, our execution of such a plan can also fail. We may find that we do not have the proper or necessary means at our disposal, or that we have bungled in using them, thus causing us to fail to achieve ends that were, in fact, achievable. I will try to address each of these potential pitfalls in the use of means/ends thinking; but given the many ways in which things can go wrong in this endeavor, it is perhaps a little more surprising when we happen to get it right.

Since means/ends arguments do not arise unless the means employed is detrimental to someone in some way, we usually do not need to search out the harm that has been done or that is likely to be done. The harm is normally the initial center of the discussion concerning whether something was (or would be) justified by performing a certain action. There are, nevertheless, a number of major issues surrounding the harm of the means which require analysis in this context. The first is the necessity of employing a harmful means to attain the end in question: Are we sure that the only road to this goal leads through this harm? Or, are there alternative routes available which would make it possible to attain the end(s) without hurting others, or at least not so badly? The second question which might be asked here concerns the seriousness of the contemplated harm. In general, the more minimal the contemplated net harm is, the more likely it is that a means/ends argument will work. But we must also take into consideration the particular identities and circumstances of those who are likely to suffer the harm. It can be argued, for example, that children should be spared certain types of harm that might justifiably be inflicted upon adults (e.g., young men of soldiering age). Thirdly, the matter of whether the "victim" participates in or acquiesces to the proposed means may also be relevant. If a potential victim, knowing the harm that is headed his or her way, directly affirms that the proposed action is somehow acceptable to him or her, then using a given means will be easier to justify because of that self-sacrifice (which could even become martyrdom, if it were to go that far). Our fourth point of concern is that when we are considering a means/ends argument, we also have to ask how likely it is that the later benefit (the "good end") will actually be achieved after the harm has been done. The more questionable the overall projected success of the enterprise is, the less likely it is that a means/ends argument will work. Finally, we need to consider how probable it is that the harm which seems to be a necessary part of the overall plan will actually be inflicted upon someone. It may not be. And the greater the chance is of the harm not happening, the more justifiable it may be to take the risk of causing that harm for the achievement of a major benefit.

When we have reviewed the potential types of errors that may occur in the use of a means, our next step is to reexamine the supposedly higher ends from several different perspectives. We need first to consider whether a given end is something moral per se: Would it be a right thing to do in and of itself (momentarily setting aside the question of what might have to be done in order to arrive at it)? Would it advance some higher moral principle? An end or objective is moral if it moves us in the direction of the ethical, and one way to determine whether or not this is the case for a given objective would be by applying our general moral guidelines. If we find that some end which we wish to achieve is not or would not be ethical in itself, then we are, in fact, not confronted with a dilemma which can be solved by the application of means/ends thinking: Not only should we not engage in the harmful action that we are contemplating using as a means, but we should also not seek the "ends" which we originally considered to be desirable. The second test of the ethical value of a given end is to weigh the positive impact it would have on others. Would it be of significant benefit to the lives of those who are being aided or would be aided? In other words, to employ means/ends thinking correctly, we need to be able to estimate the probable effects of the ends we are seeking to achieve so that we can balance them against the means we are considering using. Finally, we need to ask whether the end(s) we aim to attain might not be simultaneously beneficial and detrimental to those for whom the action may be taken. If in addition to the good things that would result (in other words, whatever it is that makes us want to achieve the objective), the ends would be likely to cause some bad things as well (in addition to the harm of the means that we are already considering), then we have to try to figure out the net impact of the ends. And if there is no perceptible net benefit to those who would be aided or advanced to some extent by the end(s), the proposal would not pass a means/ends test.

If it is probable that the end(s) aimed at would have more positive consequences than negative ones, then the final decision to be made in applying a means/ends test comes when we weigh the net benefit that was or would be gained in the achievement of the ends against the net harm that was or would be done in the application of the means (i.e., the good of the end, less the bad it may also bring, balanced against the bad of the means plus the good it may also bring to those being harmed). As with many parts of our conceptual lives, this process is not as objective or precise as is possible in making some other types of determinations (e.g., weighing a head of lettuce or balancing the number and value of presents to be given to different children on their birthdays). Nevertheless, it is not an entirely subjective process, either.

One alternative at this point in our discussion of moral decision-making might be to opt for a "greatest good for the greatest number" argument. This basic utilitarian test is not directly applicable here, however, because it balances goods against each other and does not provide for the measurement of the harm that may be necessary in order to reach some "greater" good. The type of weighing and measuring that we both do and should do when we apply a means/ends test will many times lead to the conclusion that an egregious harm done to one person may outweigh even a significant "greater good" to many others. Furthermore, the concern here is not to work out guidelines for determining the *most* ethical thing we might do in a given circumstance, but rather with deciding whether or not it is unjust to do something which, when considered by itself, would be wrong, for a supposedly higher end.

One approach we can take in trying to answer such questions is by starting with the extremes and working toward the center. Using harmful means to obtain some beneficial end should be acceptable if the means cause very little harm in the short term but lead to great benefit in the longer term, and even more so if the person who is initially harmed is included among the recipients of that later benefit. My suspicion is that we all act as if it is appropriate to proceed in such a manner, particularly in the face of some impending evil. On the other hand, a means/ends argument should not prevail if the means caused severe harm to many people and the outcome was a superficial or fleeting benefit to only one or a few other persons. (People with great power sometimes think and act as if this is ethically acceptable, but they are only deluding themselves.[11]) Therefore, when we balance means against ends, it is our obligation to try to determine whether what we are proposing to do is closer to the former extreme (likely to cause little harm for a great benefit to many), which would allow us to employ the means with a relatively clear conscience, or whether it more closely approaches the latter one (likely to cause great harm to many for only a little benefit to a few). If it is closer to the latter, then we would be morally required either to look harder for alternatives (assuming we still regarded the ends as acceptable) or to abandon our quest for those ends altogether.

How we balance means and ends will also be a function of the specific facts involved in each particular situation. No moral dilemma occurs in a vacuum, and many of them bring their own deadlines or other demands for immediate decisions and quick actions. It is one thing to employ a given means to achieve some end which is desirable but not of critical importance, but it is quite another thing if we are convinced that the end we seek is extremely crucial to us and that the only time for action is *now*. A perceived extreme immediate need for some end thought to be a high moral imperative will justify our taking more leeway in choosing and implementing the means. We might generalize by saying that the more pressing the need for the outcome, the greater the harm that can be done and condoned in its name. I would therefore underscore that we must consider the specific factual information pertinent to and the larger context of each dilemma, as these will have legitimate and important impacts on our decisions.

Another factor which may be of great significance involves our specific relationships to those who would be harmed or benefitted. The following table presents the different variables that are possible along these lines:

---

11. That attitude clearly fails all tests for justice and all standards of benevolence.

Means	Ends
Hurts me	Benefits me
Hurts individuals with whom I have a special relationship	Benefits individuals with whom I have a special relationship
Hurts other individuals	Benefits other individuals
Hurts a group to which I have a duty of loyalty	Benefits a group to which I have a duty of loyalty
Hurts other groups	Benefits other groups
Hurts everyone	Benefits everyone

For every means/ends argument, there will be at least one match in each of these columns (and possibly more) from the perspective of each person involved. A full means/ends analysis needs to take into consideration exactly who will be affected on each side of the equation from every relevant perspective.

The specific nature of the ends in question relative to the people who would benefit from them may also be significant. If the supposedly higher end is a "personal" moral matter (one of obtaining pleasure, avoiding pain, or advancing one's own self-realization), it would probably not, in many situations, be weighted as heavily as it would if the end involved the performance of one of our major interpersonal moral duties (fidelity or benevolence). Thus, the ethical nature of the objective is yet another factor that may be relevant in a means/ends balancing.

In the process of weighing means against ends, we also tend to more readily justify the use of a harmful means when it is being used to prevent some greater harm than in cases in which we are "only" trying to achieve more good. That is, prevention of an imminent evil seems to create a greater moral exigency than the advancement of a potential good—perhaps because goods can almost always be advanced in other ways. We must therefore factor into the means/ends balancing process yet another major consideration, namely, whether the end(s) sought directly conduce to positive benefits or whether they only indirectly cause positive benefits insofar as they prevent potentially negative consequences. If the latter is the case, then it is more likely that we will accept a means/ends justification.

Even though we may be comfortable with our judgments at the extremes of the moral spectrum (where little harm leads to great benefit or great harm leads to little benefit), the number of facts and factors that we must routinely juggle can make it difficult to draw a line between the permissible and the impermissible employment of some harmful means. These are, however, moral judgments that we are called upon to make. Our basic guideline should be that utilizing a harmful means is appropriate only where the net benefit of a legitimate end clearly outweighs the net harm of the means, *and*, in most cases, where the means has been or will most probably be effective in reaching the objective.[12] If we follow this guideline, we discover that egregious harm is almost never justified, while harm which amounts merely to inconvenience may often be. Clearly, there is a direct correlation between the degree of the harm which results from the implementation of the means and the degree of benefit produced by the achievement of the ends. The greater the degree of the harm caused by the means, the greater the degree of the benefit which must flow from the end(s). conversely, the less significant the benefit from achieving the end(s), the less harm we can justify doing.

There is no single criterion which can be applied in distinguishing between permissible and impermissible uses of means/ends thinking, because, as noted above, there are so many variables involved in any decision-making process. Because each of these factors can carry significant moral weight, and because individuals and their situations can vary so greatly, the decision on whether or not a specific means can be legitimately used to achieve a specific end may well depend on minor variations among them. We cannot therefore establish many general firm rules to the effect that it will or will not be morally acceptable to do "Harm X" in order to attain "End Y." The lack of

---

12. The exception here would be that in circumstances in which dire harm is imminent, greater latitude on the attainment potential is given.

hard and fast general rules does *not*, however, mean that it is impossible to obtain satisfactory answers to moral problems. Furthermore, if and when we do obtain them, we might even be able to universalize (at least to some extent) some less general rules along the following lines: It would be morally acceptable (even though it may not be *the* most moral thing to do) for actor (A) to cause this harm to the undeserving victim (V) as a necessary or appropriate means to obtain the resulting ends, because those ends are highly ethical, because the role relationships involved make it even more necessary for A to accomplish this, because the harm to be incurred by V is not egregious and thus not completely inappropriate, given the net benefit of the ends (including the fact that the ends will later indirectly benefit V by benefitting his children), and finally, because *something* has to be done relatively soon or else even greater harm would probably befall not only V but also a number of other innocent people.

Because we can also cause a great deal of unintended damage when we initiate any intentional harm, if the balancing process leaves us with a questionable result, we probably should *not* employ the means being considered. Many things that we do lead to all kinds of unanticipated consequences; and we need to remember that even if we have not foreseen an evil that follows upon our implementation of some means, we may nevertheless be morally culpable for it (particularly if we knew initially that the means we intended to use were going to be harmful to someone in some respect). Even a "small" lie supposedly told for the purpose of some higher good has, on occasion, had disastrous consequences for an innocent person. We are not omniscient, and we are not intelligent enough to be able to foresee all of the consequences of our actions. Therefore, unless the net benefit which will flow from achievement of some "higher end" is clearly and markedly greater than the net harm which is likely to result from implementation of the means, it is usually better *not* to introduce the means. The admonition, "The road to hell is paved with good intentions," has warned us for years of the dangers inherent in means/ends thinking.

In summary, when we are deciding whether to act upon a means/ends argument, we must evaluate both the proposed means and the desired ends; and then we need to balance the results. The questions to be asked include the following:

The means analysis:

1. How serious would the harm done by the means be?

2. How likely is it that the harm would actually occur?

3. How effective are the means likely to be in attaining the "good ends"?

4. What alternative means exist to attain the end(s)? And how do they compare in effectiveness and in the degree of harm they would engender?

5. Who would be harmed thereby? How innocent are they?

6. Is there any way to reduce the harm to innocent people and still achieve the ends?

7. Is there any collateral benefit to any of those who are likely to be victims of the harm?

8. Do the persons who would be harmed acquiesce, in full understanding of the ends and of the necessity of the means?

9. Could the means bring other negative or harmful consequences beyond the known likely ones? If so, how serious might they be, and how probable would their occurrence be?

10. Would the means be likely to have other positive consequences beyond the ends being directly sought?

The ends analysis:

1. Is the end morally justified? Or, if there is more than one end (such as both an immediate and a long-term one), are they all morally justified?

2. Would the ends be of significant benefit to those for whom they would be achieved? How great would those benefits be?

3. Who are the people who would be benefitted, and how great is their need for the benefit?

4. Would any other detriment (besides the anticipated harm of the means) also be likely to occur if the ends were attained?

The balancing:

1. Does the net benefit which flows from a legitimate end or ends clearly outweigh the net harm incurred by implementation of an appropriate means?

The lack of justness element thus may sometimes depend upon the outcome of a moral balancing between the harm in question and an asserted "greater good." Where an undeserved harm was done and it could not be justified by the "ends" it was supposedly used to achieve, the third element of evil would be present.

If we do decide to implement some harmful means to attain some higher end, then we are morally required to keep in mind that there are still limits on the nature and extent of the harm that we can justifiably cause. Such stopping points need to be observed closely when harm is occurring to an undeserving person or persons on the basis of means/ends thinking. The nature and degree of the harm need to be kept to the minimum levels necessary in order to accomplish the higher ends. The harm also should be terminated immediately when: (a) the ends are attained; (b) it becomes clear that the ends will not be attained through these means; (c) it becomes clear that the ends will not be of the value we anticipated, and thus would no longer outweigh the harm which would result from the implementation of the means; or (d) it becomes clear that we have underestimated the harm the means will cause and, on balance, a new analysis of the net harm which would result from implementation of the means is no longer outweighed by the projected net benefit of the probable ends. When the means are not successful enough or when they are no longer likely to be successful, we have an obligation to reexamine and reevaluate our decision-making process. A refusal or reluctance to do so can cause us to become culpable for new immoral acts—those committed while in a hot but futile pursuit of "good intentions."

Finally, when the implementation of a means/ends effort is concluded, and regardless of its success or failure, the person or persons who caused the harm to others then have the new duties of trying to ameliorate the situation and providing reparations to its undeserving victims wherever possible. That is to say, if we cause harm to undeserving persons in the name of some higher good, then at the very least, we subsequently need to try to help those whom we have harmed. The good that has been done in the larger context does not totally transform the harm that was done in the means into a good: no good can so completely digest something bad that it has consumed. We cannot merely sit back and claim that the overall ethical path we have taken absolves us from all moral responsibility, particularly from the responsibility to rectify or ameliorate a harmful situation that we have created.

Recognizing the three elements of evil—the harm, responsibility for having caused it, and its unjustness—requires knowledge not only about the issues discussed in this chapter, but also about life—about human beings and the actions in which we are engaged. While it may frequently be difficult to make these initial determinations and the moral judgments that are based upon them, confirming that what we believe we have recognized as evil is indeed evil may take even more effort and care.

4

CONFIRMING THE PRESENCE OF
EVIL AND OTHER FORMS
OF IMMORALITY

If a contemplated action seems morally questionable and, upon reflection on it, we find that only one or two of the elements of evil are present (regardless of which ones they may be and regardless of their magnitude), but that absolutely *nothing* of the third is, then we would be wrong in characterizing that act as evil or immoral, because each one of the elements is integral to such a determination. If, however, all three of these elements are present—to any extent whatsoever, then some type of immorality attaches to the action.

How do we know when each of these elements is really present? Sometimes, even when we think we have recognized them in a given context, we may still have some doubts about, for example, whether someone was really responsible for a harm, or whether a means/argument has been used legitimately. Others may express doubts about our claims, too, for they may see things somewhat differently and disagree with us in some respect or another. Hence, we are sometimes called upon to try to support and verify our conclusions.

In order to deal effectively with our own doubts and reservations and to convince others that our claims are correct, we have to consider the ways in which we can confirm assertions about moral judgments. A valid confirmation process must seek to provide effective support for conclusions about the truth or falsity of moral statements—in this case, of statements relevant to moral wrongs, like "That would really be harmful" and "This harm simply would not be justified by that benefit."

For purposes of the confirmation of statements about morality (including those about evil and other forms of immorality), we use the three main tools of ethical epistemology: reason, external authority and intuition.[1] Therefore, when seeking answers to questions about the elements of a potentially evil action, we should apply our own reasoning to it, consult others who have expertise in moral matters, and be attuned to our conscience (assuming that it is reasonably well-developed and active).

We can apply each of these types of validation not only as we consider the three elements of evil but also when we balance our observations in an effort to reach a conclusion about the morality or immorality of some action. Rationally, we can review the factors involved and determine whether, on the basis of the information that is available to us, sufficient evidence exists to support a conclusion. We can also consult current or historical external authorities on each of these matters at any time; and we can "listen" for any intuitive input we may have.

Conscience is quite useful in confirming final conclusions about wrong actions. Most of us have recognized and internalized consider-able ethical guidance on moral negatives (perhaps even more than on moral positives); and we are able to respond almost automatically with regard to some wrong actions. (Indeed, the alacrity with which conscience directs us is a phenomenon worth reflection.) This guidance helps us both validate and verify many assertions and positions about good and evil. People who possess a well-developed moral conscience can have a fairly high degree of confidence in their tentative conclusions about the truth of a negative assertion like "That is wrong," or "What you intend to do would be evil."

Similarly, we all know people in whose moral judgment we place a great deal of trust. If we can obtain their considered opinions about

---

1. In *Being Ethical* I discussed the epistemology of moral knowledge and how these tools are used to confirm truth about what is ethical.

a proposed judgment on the immorality of a given action, we are justified in having greater confidence in our conclusion if it coincides with those opinions, and less confidence if it does not. Even if we are not able to lay out the particulars of a given case before a respected moral authority, we can often still refer to their teachings for direction and support.

If we want to have substantial assurance in our conclusions about potentially immoral actions, however, we should apply all three of these epistemological methods to our analysis of each of the three individual elements of evil and to the conclusions that we draw following a balanced review of those determinations.

With regard to the first element, which is harm, while we may seek rational support for a conclusion on the basis of the factual information that we possess about a given circumstance, we often initially react reflexively and thus essentially intuitively. When we see someone gasping for air, for example, we do not feel any need to think about it; we intuitively realize that the person is suffering harm. Our intuitive capacity is developed and refined as we learn about things that have harmed us or that could have harmed us in the past and as we empathize with others whose well-being is in jeopardy. Underlying the development of this empathy is a logically analyzable progression of insights—an argument in abbreviated form. We may be thinking, for example: "Oxygen deprivation is harmful," "This act is depriving someone of oxygen," "Therefore, this act is harmful." On other occasions, however, we may want or need to rely heavily on other people in drawing our conclusions about the nature of the harm involved in a given situation, as when a first-hand witness describes over the telephone the apparent suffering of a faraway victim, or when a physician explains specifically how and why an injured person was in pain.

The same things are true with the second element of evil, namely responsibility for the harm done to another. We can apply reason to be sure that we review each of the various questions that need to be considered before drawing any conclusion about it. But we can also intuit moral responsibility, and we can gain valuable insight about all factors involved in this element from those with expertise in moral matters. The need for input from others regarding responsibility for a harm may become particularly important with regard to a conclusion that a perpetrator "should have known" ahead of time that a certain harmful result would be likely to ensue from the action taken.

The third element—the lack of justness of the harm—requires the same types of analysis for the purpose of confirmation. We can rationally gather and review those facts which might aid us in ruling out exceptions that would make a harm "just"—legitimate punishment, self-defense, instruction or some other benefit to the victim or to others. Sometimes we can also intuitively understand the lack of justness of a harm, and we can factor in the assessments and opinions from others on these valuation issues, as well.

As the final step in this confirmation process, we should review the separate conclusions drawn with respect to each of the three elements. An appeal to the intuition which accompanies an active and developed conscience can be useful at this point as well. Does it feel or seem correct to conclude that this act is or would be morally wrong? Similarly, since ethics is primarily a social activity, it is important to be apprized of the ethical judgments of others whose views are trustworthy. Generally speaking, the greater the level of concurrence among morally-attuned people about the wrongfulness of some action, the more likely it is that the action is indeed wrong.

An alternative framework may also be of assistance to us in these efforts. It involves looking not at the specific elements of evil, but rather for more indirect indications of the moral direction being taken with the action in question. As we make our initial determinations about the morality of a given action, we can verify their accuracy by asking whether or not that action leads us toward one or more of the negative endpoints of a moral continuum. Actions that move us away from the positive side of such a spectrum and toward the negative (e.g., those which break down our discipline vis-a-vis pleasure and pain, or those which might diminish our capacity for self-realization, loyalty or benevolence) are at least questionable with regard to their morality; and insights of this sort into the consequences of an action measured along these continuums can be relied upon to further clarify for us its ethical or unethical nature.

When we move toward the ethical in the continuum that deals with issues of personal pleasure and pain, our principal moral task is generally to exercise some degree of restraint and to avoid excess and/or deficiency. Both indulgence and deprivation represent lack of moderation. When we abandon the middle ground, we can cause substantial harm, both to ourselves and to others.

While it can be said that we may often deserve the harms that come to us as a result of our engaging in excess, our culpability in this area usually stems more from a negligent disregard for the harmful consequences these pursuits are likely to have on others, and also from the bad habits and character defects that may develop as a result of prolonged self-indulgence. As we choose more pleasure and less pain for ourselves regardless of the consequences to others, we tend to ignore our interpersonal ethical responsibilities.

Negative movement along this continuum—particularly toward excessive pleasure—tends to correlate directly with numerous subsequent immoral actions. Personal pleasure is a powerful force in our lives (e.g., lust and greed do motivate most of us, at least some of the time and to some extent). And, when we head in the wrong way down this path, we often do not take into consideration the consequences of our actions on others. Thus, if some type of pleasure has become a matter of consuming importance, how our pursuit of that pleasure may impact someone else may be an issue that gets set aside in the course of that pursuit. If we want a given pleasure badly and may be prevented from obtaining it by others who seem to be "in the way," then we often forge ahead obsessively. Greed and covetousness can come to rule the day. In the initial stages of our search for pleasure, we may have absolutely no intention of causing harm to others. We may, in fact, only be intent on overcoming or removing those things which impede us. But we often become careless when we are strongly focused on attaining such objectives, and, in the process, we can cause substantial harm to others by our selfish choices.

We can begin answering the question of whether an action either is moving us or would move us toward the negative end of the moral continuum dealing with pain and pleasure issues by looking for vices that are related to it. Evil is often the product of vicious actions, so a sort of "guilt by association" argument may be quite valid here. While it can also be the case that evil is the product of something else (i.e., negligence), vice leads us to do things that can be, and most frequently are, evil or otherwise immoral. In other words, where we discern the presence of some vice, particularly one which goes uncorrected over a long period of time, it is likely that we will also see some morally wrong action resulting from it at some point.

Vices relevant to matters driven by personal pleasures and pains derive from excesses or deficiencies. Recurring patterns of such excessive or deficient behavior therefore point to either the presence or potential emergence (or deepening) of some vice, and thus to the likelihood of immoral consequences flowing from it.

While totally abstaining from pleasure and neglecting to avoid pain may constitute a vice (of deficiency) and may lead to problematic developments, the vices associated with excess are more troublesome. Specific vices that lead to excess in the pursuit of pleasure include self-indulgence, profligacy, immoderation, gluttony, lust and avarice. Conversely, the vices associated with excessive avoidance of pain cause us to yield unthinkingly to fear and give in too quickly to the impulse to flee. They include cowardice, timidity, fearfulness and excessive apprehensiveness. Where such inclinations are present, there is a greater likelihood that the action under discussion has moved the agent toward the negative end of this moral continuum. Observing such a fact can help confirm our hypothesis about the presence of evil in a given situation.

The goal of self-realization provides a second approach to the discussion and analysis of moral human action. It, too, relies on the insight that one of the essential features of sound moral judgment is balance, and excess in either direction moves us toward the negative end of its continuum. An imbalance in the direction of deficiency or deprivation stems from an indifference to our potential for self-realization or from a tendency toward self-destructiveness (which, of course, if accomplished successfully would permanently end our ability to become self-realized). An imbalance in the other direction (perhaps more common in our time) involves excessive efforts to accomplish too much as an individual, to the exclusion of any consideration for others; and it is thus contrary to our obligations of fidelity and benevolence. When we seek to attain some specific personal objective as part of an effort in self-realization, and we do so without giving any thought to the consequences that our actions might have for others, our selfishness may lead us to harm them unjustifiably. While we may sometimes intentionally harm others in our efforts to become self-realized (e.g., by trying to sabotage the efforts of a competitor), more often harm done to others in this area originates from responses which derive from character-defects—from things like laziness or indifference on the one hand to selfishness or excessive personal ambition on the other.

Vices that are associated with the negative end of the self-realization continuum and that could therefore be relevant to an effort to confirm or refute the fact that some unjust harm had been done to another include: excessive pride or ambition, egotism, vanity, arrogance, conceit, excessive humility, greed, envy, pessimism, self-deception and pretentiousness; disgruntlement, obsequiousness, servility, despondency and gloominess; weakness, disorderliness, sloth and complacency; and carelessness, imprudence, rebelliousness, anger, recklessness, impetuosity, impulsiveness and inflexibility. When any of these evidences itself in the context of some questionable or problematic action, then we may have found support for a conclusion that something wrong may already have happened, or is likely to happen.

A third approach to ethical problem-solving is to think in terms of the general virtue of fidelity. It is composed of two major parts: (1) loyalty (to God, to a social group, and to individuals with whom we are involved in primary relationships); and (2) honesty, or adherence to our word. The negative end of this moral spectrum would therefore contain infidelity, including disloyalty (to God, to a social group, or to important individuals in our lives) and dishonesty.

In order to discern whether an action which we suspect to be immoral would move its agent in a negative direction along this moral continuum, we first need to identify the major groups and important individuals in our lives to whom we owe special duties of loyalty, and then we need to understand and outline those duties.

While personal dishonesty is generally not difficult to recognize (although self-deception sometimes clouds our thinking), recognizing dishonesty in others requires more skill and practice. Fortunately, however (in this context), experience does indeed seem to be the best teacher.

We can be disloyal to ourselves, and we can also be dishonest with ourselves; but when we do something harmful which amounts to a breach of our duty of fidelity, usually someone else is on the receiving end of it. In other words, if, in a situation in which some action is necessary, I fail to act as a good friend and my friend is harmed by my failure, then I would have breached my duty of loyalty to him. Similarly, while dishonesty may sometimes have a benevolence objective (e.g., saying "You are going to be fine" to an accident victim when the outcome is unclear or possibly adverse), our lies are often actually intended either to cause harm to others or to evade justifiable harm to ourselves without regard for the well-being of others.

We are more likely to cause unjust harm to others when we are disloyal and/or dishonest than we are when we are "simply" breaching our personal moral duties (of making appropriate plea-sure/pain responses and of pursuing self-realization), because our duty to fidelity involves our personal interactions with those with whom we have relationships of primary import. That is, if we are doing something which violates this obligation, then others are the ones who would primarily be hurt.

The vices encompassed by disloyalty include disobedience, treachery, selfishness, alienation, intolerance, disrespectfulness, unreliability, stubbornness, obstinacy, rebelliousness, irresponsibility and zealotry; and those encompassed by dishonesty include deceit-fulness, phoniness, hypocrisy, disingenuousness and insincerity. If in reviewing a conclusion we have reached preliminarily about the immorality of some action, we become aware of the presence of any such vice motivating that action—and thus become aware that the agent is moving in a negative direction along the fidelity continuum, the validity of our preliminary conclusion will have been supported.

Lastly, benevolence can also serve as a basis for adjudicating the morality of human actions. In order to become fully benevolent, we would need to do not only what is required in the lowest level of development of this virtue (not causing unjust harm to others), but also in the midrange (avoiding injustice and actively doing justice), and in the highest level (pro-actively doing charity). Analyzing actions under this important approach to the ethical requires that we focus primarily on how well or how poorly we treat others. An action that treats others poorly or uncharitably represents movement toward the negative end of this spectrum.

To determine what our duties of benevolence are with respect to specific people and groups, we have to know what their "due" is. What kind of treatment are they entitled to from us? When we fail to give any other person his or her "due" in circumstances in which it is owed, we are in breach of our duty of benevolence toward that person. At a minimum, other people are owed basic respect as human beings. Among other things, they are also entitled to what they have earned, as well as to a fair share of the resources and opportunities of the groups to which they belong. Although we have this basic obligation of general benevolence (and fairness) to every other person with whom we may interact, our concurrent duty of loyalty obligates us to an even higher level of benevolence toward certain people (e.g., family members). And, when we fail to give someone his or her "due," we can scarcely say that we are comporting ourselves ethically vis-a-vis that person; and we may, by such an omission, be acting unethically.

Vices whose presence may help us decide whether an action could be leading someone in the wrong direction with respect to benevolence include those which are based in lack of charity (e.g., lack of generosity, stinginess, coldness), those which derive from failure to be just (including intolerance, unjustness and carelessness), and those emanating from injustice (such as incivility, disrespectfulness, covetousness and unfairness). Vices which may motivate us to cause harm to others intentionally include cruelty, maliciousness, depravity, malevolence and spitefulness.

Discerning the ethical direction of an action may be relevant and useful to any conclusions we may draw about it. I am therefore suggesting that, after we make our determinations about the morality of a given action using the epistemological means discussed above (i.e., reasoning about it, appealing to authoritative interpretations and precedents, and allowing our intuition to "speak" to us), we can further verify the correctness of our conclusions by trying to determine toward which end of the moral spectrums the action would cause us to move with respect to the four general approaches to the ethical set out above.

The following examples demonstrate the application of the verification processes described in this chapter:

Example A. You are walking down a street by yourself when you see a person lying before you. That person appears to have been robbed and beaten unconscious. What should you *not* do?

If our objective is to try to avoid doing something wrong, we must first attempt not to cause any harm. Sometimes this may be difficult due to circumstances, but often harm is the element of evil that we can most readily avert.

We could begin in this situation, for example, by choosing not to beat or rob that person ourselves, and we could also take measures to ensure that he does not incur any further injuries as a result of some negligence on our part (e.g., tripping over him). If we cause more pain, or if we steal something from that person—both of which would in almost every instance be unjust—then we would be committing an act that involved both the first and second elements of evil.

With regard to the element of unjustness, however, the example above is perhaps inadequately detailed in some respects; because in some unusual circumstances and on rare occasions, doing additional harm to an apparent victim may not be wrong. If the person lying in the street is feigning injury as part of an attempt to trap and rob an unwary good Samaritan, then harm that is caused to that person as part of legitimate self-defense would not be unjustly dealt to him. Another type of justifiable harm done to a person in such a situation might include appropriate forms of punishment (e.g., a case in which he was the initial robber who had been injured in self defense by his intended victim, and you were considering recovering something that was originally stolen by him with the intention of returning it to its owner). Another possible consideration relating to the justness question would be whether any "higher goods" might warrant inflicting further harm upon this person (e.g., if both the passerby and the "victim" were wartime enemies, and the "victim" was a spy who, upon recovering consciousness, would provide critical intelligence that could devastate the defenses of the group associated with the passerby).

Even though such exceptions may exist, however, the rarity of these examples supports the general conclusion that we may draw from our reflections here: Directly causing additional harm to someone who has apparently already suffered such an adversity will almost always be fundamentally unjust. This conclusion is and would be supported in turn by reason, by intuition, and by credible moral authorities. It also is the determination that would avoid some of the unbenevolence vices and that would not head the passerby toward the negative end of the benevolence spectrum.

A full discussion of what we should not do in such a case cannot end with that generalization, however. The more important and more interesting question to be raised here is *not* whether we should continue to beat a man who is down, but rather whether we must try to help him, if we are to avoid engaging in an immoral act by omission. While a strong consensus would exist for the proposition that our duty of loyalty would require that we assist a son or brother if he were lying injured in a ditch, not everyone would claim that helping a stranger in a similar situation is a moral imperative.[2]

It is essential to remember that while our benevolence duties to the public at large begin with the duty not to cause harm, they are followed by the general duty not to do injustice, and then by the duty to do justice, and lastly, in some instances, by the obligation to engage in acts of charity. If we are in a position to help someone who is injured and lying by the side of the road and we do not do so, then we are clearly failing to fulfill both of our highest duties to act benevolently (having neglected our obligations to do both charity and justice). However, we are not now trying to establish what we need to do in order to be ethical, but rather what we need to avoid doing in order not to be unethical. Do we harm others further if, upon observing that they have already suffered some harm or injury, we choose not to help ameliorate their situation? Do we do injustice to others if we ignore them when they are in need? I would propose that the answer to both of these questions is "yes."

---

2. Despite the fact that we are all at least distant cousins, if either evolution or most religious tradition is correct.

Failure to help someone in need is an error of omission, rather than one of commission. If a toddler has wandered away from an incapacitated mother and is in the street in front of us and a bus a half block away would pose no immediate danger to us if we were to take the trouble to pluck the child from the street, and we choose to merely stand and watch the child be run over by the bus, we are indeed morally culpable. Such a failure to act may not constitute a criminal action, but it is obviously morally wrong.

We are similarly culpable whenever we allow harm being suffered by others to be perpetuated; and insofar as we neglect to stop it, we may become responsible for it—at least in those cases in which it was indeed in our power to halt it and we clearly failed to do so. If the man lying in the ditch would suffer for five more hours in the absence of my help, but only for two more hours if I would provide him with assistance, would I not be responsible, at least to some extent, for the additional suffering to which he would be subject if I chose to ignore him? In this example, we have the presence of harm (suffering unnecessarily prolonged), responsibility for it (through the intentional failure to provide assistance), and a lack of justification for the failure to act (assuming none of the types of exceptions discussed above would apply[3]). From these determinations, we can conclude that ignoring him and his plight would almost inevitably be immoral and cause us to drift away from the positive end of the benevolence continuum. It is also likely that one or more of the vices that are related to the benevolence spectrum would be present if we were to ignore such an injured man (e.g., lack of generosity, disrespectfulness or maliciousness).

If we appeal to external authorities in an attempt to adjudicate this question, the great religious and ethical traditions advise us not only that helping others in distress is right and necessary, but also that failing to help others in dire need is wrong. Many contemporary moral theorists would, I expect, concur in this. Most people would also feel guilty doing nothing under such circumstances. Neglecting

---

3. In addition, even if we could not offer direct assistance for some good reason, as in the case of a physical infirmity, or if we were afraid to do so because of potentially hazardous circumstances, we could at least notify others who could do so.

someone who is obviously in need would be incompatible with the dictates of an active conscience, and moral intuition would likely cause us to feel at least momentary pangs of guilt at the thought of neglecting a man who has been injured and is in a helpless state. Therefore, in this example, not only should we not directly cause additional harm to the victim, but we should also not fail to come to his assistance.

Example B. You belong to the dominant racial and cultural group in your country. Your group has dominated the other racial and cultural groups there for a long time, but the leaders of your group are worried about new challenges to that domination, and they are making plans to strengthen their control by planting "disinformation" about the other groups. As part of your job, you are directed to take part in that effort. What should you *not* do?

This example allows us to explore the limits of our duty of fidelity to a social group. When can we be morally required to harm others in furtherance of our own group's agenda, given the fact that, generally speaking, furthering the interests of our primary groups is a fundamental loyalty obligation? The case also raises the issue of when one should or should not commit a harmful act for a supposedly higher good.

It is, I believe, readily apparent that we are conceding both that some harm is being done in this case (Example B), and that some agent is known to be responsible for it. It is also clear that the intended harm would be unjust to the intended victims themselves, because they would continue to be deprived of a fair share of the resources and opportunities of the group. The real issue here is therefore whether or not the potentially "higher good" (of the maintenance of your group's hold on power) justifies harm caused or furthered by an immoral action (dishonesty).

As history, sociology and anthropology demonstrate, there are many reasons for regarding group betterment as a justified higher end relative to many lesser harms. However, while, for example, lying can sometimes be a diplomatically efficacious means of advancing important group objectives, it would not, at least in this example, be a morally sound way in which to proceed. The means/ends justification offered in this case would not allow us to escape culpability, since the end, namely, unjust domination of one group by another, is morally wrong from every relevant perspective, even when we consider only the dominant group.

A review of the proposed "ends" in this case under the aegis of the four approaches to analyzing ethical action outlined previously supports this conclusion. Groups as well as individuals seek pleasure and avoid pain, but the pleasures to which the unjust dominance of one group over another leads are unbalanced and excessive. Being an oppressive group and/or actively participating in such a group are also negative rather than positive forms of self-realization. While loyalty to our main groups may lend a patina of morality to such an enterprise, excessive loyalty, or loyalty to an unworthy group or cause, is by no means a virtue; and zealotry is patently vicious. Similarly, reflection on this case in light of our general obligation to act benevolently reveals that depriving people in other groups of their "due" is immoral. When faced with such a situation, we would also probably be able to recognize intolerance, unfairness and spitefulness among the vices that would accompany any such action; and we would likely see, as well, movement toward the negative ends of several moral continuums.

Listening for input from one's conscience and seeking counsel from neutral external authorities should help confirm this conclusion. The action being proposed here would not pass any balanced review by ethical authorities, nor is it the type of thing that an active conscience could legitimately condone, particularly when the situation was assessed in a neutral context.

From all relevant perspectives, therefore, proceeding with such a disinformation campaign would amount to participating in an unethical enterprise, and it would thus be something in which we should not engage.

Example C. Your best friend has asked your advice. Your friend has information about a corrupt official and wants to know whether she should blow the whistle on her. Because of the nature of the corrupt official's friends, reporting her wrongdoing would almost certainly cause them to seek revenge, and they

would probably be successful at that and cause your friend substantial harm. What should you *not* do?

This third case illustrates the types of decisions we have to make vis-a-vis specific people to whom we are obligated in special relationships. To analyze this example, we first have to identify and classify the various actors. A good friendship imposes special loyalty duties upon us. In other words, we normally have to extend ourselves more to and for our friends than to or for strangers. (For purposes of this example, the corrupt official can be presumed to be a stranger.)

The friend described here could be hurt in a variety of ways if she were to report the corruption. Such harm would clearly be unjust—she would not have done anything to warrant it; indeed, she should receive praise and other rewards for doing the right thing. The official could also be harmed in turn; but, given that she is engaged in some wrongdoing, the harm which she might incur would probably be her "due" (assuming an appropriate level of a response in self-defense or punishment). The third individual who has become involved in the situation (the friend whose advice is being asked) is also facing potential personal harm—the loss of or injury to her friend. In addition, the situation could also entail some sort of harm to third parties as a result of the official's continued wrongdoing. If, based on the offered advice, the friend decided not to blow the whistle, then both of the friends might bear some degree of responsibility for any injury or damage that might be incurred by innocent third parties.

Loyalty to a friend poses a dilemma because of concern for her physical safety, on the one hand, and for her moral state on the other. Some more details about this situation would have to be obtained before it would be clear what the best advice would be. Specifically how, for example, could one minimize personal exposure and at the same time stop the progress of an immoral enterprise? Once again, however, we are not presently looking for the best or most ethical alternative, but rather for what it would not be ethical for the adviser to do.

It would not be right in such a situation to advise a friend to ignore the problem and take no action. Acting responsibly would entail trying to assist that friend in becoming self-realized as a good person. However, our loyalty obligations to a friend would also dictate that some thought be given to ways in which potential harm might be avoided or minimized. Loyalty to the group in question that would continue to be harmed by the official's corruption would also prohibit inaction, as would the responsibility to act benevolently toward third parties who might become victims of the actions of the corrupt official.

A choice to advise a friend to do nothing in such a situation would suggest the presence of several of the vices of disloyalty and dishonesty, not only to the friend but also to the group in question, as well as vices in the benevolence area (like disrespectfulness and coldheartedness) toward other individuals who might be affected. But unless the risk of severe harm to a friend were very high and little hope existed for the successful outcome of the whistle-blowing effort, advising her to avoid doing her ethical duty—in this case, to put a halt to an immoral undertaking—would, in and of itself, be an unethical choice and move the "adviser" toward the negative ends of several moral spectrums. And once again, especially if put in a neutral context, both conscience and moral authorities would support this outcome.

Even when we feel that we have confirmed that something evil or immoral has happened or is likely to happen, our philosophical labors are not finished; the work of recognizing evil has yet another important step. Just as not all ethical actions have the same merit, so, also, not all immoral acts have the same "demerit." Some wrongs are clearly worse that others, and how we should appropriately react to different kinds and degrees of immorality depends upon how wrong an action may be. The next chapter will address the question of such kinds and degrees of immorality.

5

DEGREES OF EVIL AND OTHER
FORMS OF IMMORALITY

I f we find that something immoral has occurred, is occurring or is impending, then, in order to formulate a considered response to it, we also need to be able to establish the degree of its immorality. Some things are clearly morally worse than others, or else we would react to a spiteful sarcastic comment the same way we do to a gruesome murder.

The first step in recognizing approximately where along the negative end of the ethical continuum a given unjust harmful act should be properly placed is to consider the degree to which each of the three elements of evil is present in it. The more injurious the harm proves to be, or the more substantial the degree of responsibility assigned to the agent, or the more that justness is lacking, the more likely it is that the act will be deemed to be worse than other immoral acts for which these things are not the case.

Analyzing the nature and extent of the harm done is probably the easiest part of this task. A strong consensus can usually be obtained at least on what the most damaging kinds of harm are and on what the most inconsequential kinds of harm are. While occasionally there are complicating issues like some types of individual differences (e.g., special sensitivities that heighten the degree of harm suffered from a particular type of injurious action) or like some kinds of group differences (e.g., special harms that occur to members of a racial group that has suffered from considerable discrimination in the past), we should be able to agree on many basic evaluations of comparative harms (e.g., that a bruised arm is almost always less harmful than a broken arm).

In determining the degree of harm, we apply our own experience and memories about the types of things that have hurt us comparatively more or less. Making comparisons is a natural and almost reflexive mental function. We do this before making many of our choices (e.g., "I think the chicken will taste better than the fish tonight"). We also do this when we consider harms that we want to avoid. Each of us has extensive experience with harms, and we almost automatically make choices about which harms we will assiduously attempt to avoid and which ones we would be inclined to allow ourselves to suffer if the effort involved in avoiding them would be too great.

Before we make an important judgment about the relative degree of a harm, we often seek the input of others who have good powers of observation and a credible moral sense. That we are fairly good collectively in making these evaluations is reflected in such things as the standard schedules of recompense that we have adopted for payments for diverse types of injuries through workers' compensation laws, under which different monetary awards are given for injuries to different body parts, along an accepted scale.

The second element, responsibility, can vary in degree from a "clearly responsible" level down to a "barely responsible" one. We attach the highest degree of moral responsibility to actions in which the accused harmdoer clearly intended to cause the act, clearly knew that the harm would result from the action, and clearly had self-control sufficient to have allowed him or her to avoid causing the harm. We ascribe lesser degrees of moral responsibility when we really did not intend to do the harmful act but were responsible for it in some other way (such as through our negligence), when we did not actually know that the act would cause harm (but should have known it), or when we barely had enough self-control to be able to avoid doing it.

When we consider the degree of responsibility to attach to an evil act, we usually focus on the reason why the agent did it. Intentional actions are, by definition, the result of the exercise of free will; they happened because the actor wanted them to. But there are sometimes other reasons why people may be responsible for unjust harm.

Intentionality is made up of two principal parts. In analyzing it, we consider both whether the person intended the act that led to the harm and whether the person intended to harm someone by engaging in the action.

When someone intends to cause unjustified harm to another by a given action and succeeds, that person is clearly blameworthy. Our strongest moral reactions are and should be reserved for such incidents, since people who engage in these types of activities are generally the most dangerous to society. People who may be inclined to cause such harm purposefully need to be deterred, if at all possible, or else their bad intentions will become fulfilled ever more frequently. Consequently, we have to act promptly and competently against intentional wrongdoing if we want to provide and maintain useful self-defense and effective justice.

We recognize that someone intends to do a harmful act first through any direct verbal and nonverbal admissions about it. When we aim to cause harm to others, however, our tendency is to dissimulate about our true intentions in some way. Therefore, we often have to look for indirect indicators and consider them in the context of our understandings about how and why people act in certain ways.

Deciphering the intention of some agent to act in a certain way is usually easier than deciphering a direct intention to cause harm, in part because the latter is, in itself, often blameworthy and thus frequently better hidden. In addition, we cannot always know what the consequences of our actions will be; and thus, while meaning to engage in some action, we may not be intending to cause any harm whatsoever. We are therefore more likely to have to deduce the intention to cause harm from indirect or circumstantial evidence than we are to find a stated intention to do a harmful act.

How can we identify intentional evildoers who are skillful at hiding their objectives? When confronted with individuals who may have engaged in some evil action, we have to evaluate both their statements (or their silence) and their actions (or their inaction), and then deduce whether they really intended to engage in the action and thereby cause the harm, or whether in fact they did not. To do this we have to weigh the probable truth or falsehood of their statements of intention in conjunction with: (a) what we know about people generally; (b) what we know about these people specifically; and (c) what we can observe about directions or tendencies in their behavior. We should carefully consider whether they have anything to gain from their actions (or omissions), because if obvious benefits were to accrue to those persons following the commission of the harmful act, at least some suspicion would be cast on any claims they might make to the contrary. We have to figure out, as best we can, what the perpetrators were doing (or not doing) prior to and while taking the action, and then infer, as best we can, what they were thinking (or not thinking) when they engaged in the harmful act. To answer the first question ("What was being done?"), we need relevant information about observable actions, which is best obtained from a good witness or witnesses. To answer the second question ("What was being thought?"), we need experience in dealing with people and a general understanding of them. It also helps immensely if we have experience in dealing with the particular person or persons in question and some familiarity with their attitudes toward life and social behaviors. Finally, we should also take into consideration the fact that there might be still other explanations for their actions; and, in cases when one has been offered by the perpetrators, we should try to determine whether it can withstand a skeptical examination.

If we can fairly conclude, either from express statements of intention or from other statements or actions, that a person intends both the act that causes unjust harm and the harm that results from the act, then the highest level of intentionality may be assigned to the agent of the harm, for purposes of assessing the degree of moral responsibility which accrues to an action.

Thus far, our discussion of reasons for causing harm has focused primarily upon harm which is intentionally caused. But, in addition to this, we need to consider two other major reasons for engaging in harmful action, because an action may not involve any intentionality at all or may involves only partial intentionality (the agent meant the act but not the harm, or he meant the harm but not the act).

Character defects and negligence are thus also at issue here.[1] In both of these types of cases, it can usually be said that we "should have known" that the act would cause harm (as opposed to actually knowing that it would). In both of these types of cases we are culpable primarily because we could and should have avoided engaging in the action, and hence also causing the harm.

We identify character defects based upon our personal experience, through observation and lifelong learning, and by relying on our collective assessments of such matters. Character defects are habitual. They are therefore almost automatic or reflexive patterns of feeling and thinking which tend to lead us into doing things that are wrong. Furthermore, they are directly related to our vices and may be described, to some extent, as ingrained vices. I suspect that most if not all of us have from time to time felt the emotional weakness that tempts us toward the vices that can lead us to commit evil acts. We know of problems with character defects because we all have them or have had them, to a greater or lesser extent. As perpetrators of wrongs or as victims, we learn the hard way about such defects and their negative consequences. Character can be built, however. When our parents told us to share our toys, they were trying to help us develop a good habit and prevent or break the bad habit of selfishness; for the latter, if it takes root, can frequently lead us to cause unjust harm to others (for, as we are all aware, it takes but a single moment under the influence of one of our ingrained vices in which we react—in anger or jealousy, for example—and cause harm to others).

Character defects have certain earmarks which enable us to recognize them when they are present. These include things like an acknowledged indifference to basic moral principles, a high degree of self-absorption, and a gross insensitivity toward others. But because it is not the case that only people of a generally bad moral character act unjustly and cause harm to others, but also other people who seem to have a sound character, we need to be able to recognize isolated or temporarily dominant vices and character defects. And we can usually know whether a harmful act resulted

---

1. See the works of Milo and Kekes, *supra*.

from an isolated or infrequently tolerated vice (or a character defect) or from a "well-developed" one by consulting our personal experience and the experience of others who are knowledgeable about human nature. (E.g., "I believe that Joe's long-held envy caused him to hurt Frank by telling the lie that led to Frank's financial loss, because I *know* what envy is, and because I know how Joe's been feeling about this for a long time.") Other people can not only assist us in understanding these basic concepts and how they are rooted in our emotions, but they can also advise us on particular incidents. Such advice and input may help us develop a better understanding of human moral character, as well.

The specific judgments that we make about the degree of immorality that attaches to an act can sometimes be influenced by a person's general character. In other words, having a good reputation matters. If those who are acquainted with the person whose actions are under review believe that he or she does not have significant character defects, he or she may get the benefit of the doubt in a debate about his or her culpability. If, on the other hand, that person is believed to have a generally bad character or to have an extremely strong character defect that may have led to his or her commission of the unjust act, then he or she will probably receive the "harm of the doubt" in that judgment.

In addition to being held morally responsible for harmful actions because of our bad intentions or character defects, we may also be considered culpable on the basis of negligence and carelessness. Care and attentiveness always require focus and effort, but at times competing demands may make it extremely difficult to maintain such focus. If we have to drive fourteen hours in one day to get to a destination by a particular time, especially if we are tired or emotionally diverted, we may do things at the wrong place or time which could cause an accident (e.g., straying into another lane is often not a problem, but sometimes another vehicle will be there). In the routine of everyday life, we sometimes drop things, run into doors, cut ourselves, etc. Part of being alive seems to be causing or contributing to accidents (usually—and fortunately—injuring only ourselves). When, however, carelessness on our part leads to an accident that harms another person, we are morally culpable. Had we exercised the level of self-control of which we are normally capable, and had we been as careful as we usually are able to be, the accident and subsequent injury or damage would not have occurred. If we could have prevented the harm if we had really been trying hard enough to do so, then the unjust harm that we caused to another person would be our fault.

We can assess cases involving negligence and carelessness in the same ways we do those adjudicated on the basis of intentionality or character defects. We directly recognize carelessness because at times we ourselves have been careless, as have others around us. And we know the consequences of carelessness because we have seen them. We can obtain valuable insights from others on issues of culpable carelessness, as well. These make it possible for us to understand what normally constitutes caution and thereby to be able to apply consensual standards for responsible behavior in our assessments of this type of culpability. The insights of others are also valuable with regard to the degree of caution that should have been exercised by an individual who may or may not have caused an unjust harm negligently, as well as with regard to the degree of negligence that was involved (e.g., gross or slight).

The degree of moral responsibility someone bears for an unjust harmful act that they have committed greatly affects the degree of overall culpability we assign to them. True malevolence may come in several different shades and varieties; but regardless of its nuances, it is assigned the highest degree of blame in this element. Moral indifference follows, which is the stance of those who do not care whether their actions cause harm to others or whether their actions prevent other people from receiving their due. Substantially unmotivated by any benevolent concern for others, those who are morally indifferent may cause significant harm because the consequences of their actions largely remain unreflected upon as they move through life. And such a persistent and deeply embedded lack of concern for others causes more problems, and would almost always receive more blame, than a temporary attitude of indifference to others. At the lowest level of the scale on which we measure responsibility for causing harm are occasional failures to be careful and thus actions committed in culpable negligence (e.g., those which occur for some physical reason, such as fatigue, or for a mental one, such as boredom).

The spectrum which underlies our analysis of the third element—the lack of justness of a harm—runs from grossly unjust to scarcely unjust. Exactly how unjust a harmful action may be is sometimes difficult to determine because these can be matters of fairly close questions. We may find that we have to address, for example, whether the harm could actually somehow also benefit the "victim," or whether a certain type of act merits any punishment at all due to evolving community standards on the issue. Nevertheless, degrees of the lack of justness of immoral acts will range from the totally unjust to the slightly more probable that not that something was unjust.

If there is initially no apparent issue about the unjustness of a harmful action to another, and if no reasonable argument can be framed contending that the harm was justly done, then the event will be properly ascribed to the "totally unjust" end of this scale. If there is, however, some ambiguity in a given case, then in trying to resolve it, we should ask the following questions:

a. If the argument being put forward concerns appropriate punish-ment, would the imposition and degree of the proposed sanction be clearly right, or only barely so? Or, conversely, would it be only barely wrong, or obviously so?

b. If the argument concerns self-defense, would the basis for and the manner and degree of that defense be clearly justified, or barely so; or would it be barely wrong, or clearly so?

c. If the argument concerns what might be deemed necessary instruction, is that instruction and how it is proposed to be accomplished clearly right or barely right, or barely wrong or clearly so?

d. If the argument concerns some ultimate benefit to the "victim," is the benefit itself and the contention that it outweighs the harm clearly right or barely so, or barely wrong or clearly so?

e. If the argument concerns some justifiable greater benefit to others, has the balancing of the means and ends been done in a way which is clearly right or barely so, or   barely wrong or clearly so?

As we answer these questions by drawing on the various sources of expertise in moral matters that are available to us, we will be able to make better judgments about the comparative degrees of unjustness which should attach to any given action.

Before making a final assessment in any specific case, however, we need to take into consideration the fact that it can be affected by a number of things which may be offered as defenses. People who have committed immoral acts frequently attempt to downgrade the degree of their seriousness in order to diminish any consequences to which they, as culpable perpetrators, may be subject.

While defenses can be offered with regard to all three of the elements, as we try to determine the blameworthiness of some agent, we may find that many of them are concerned with the element of responsibility and turn on the issue of self-control. Of the commonly attempted defenses, there are several general varieties; but they all try to lead to the conclusion that the suspected wrongdoer did not have the capacity to avoid causing the harm, for one reason or another. There are psychological defenses (e.g., some sort of mental illness or defect), sociological defenses (e.g., bad surroundings or bad training), biological defenses (e.g., genetic problems or deficiencies), religious defenses (e.g., "The devil made me do it"), and political defenses (e.g., anger at oppression, legitimate or otherwise). Some of these arguments we sometimes accept; and as a consequence, we ascribe lesser degrees of culpability to the agent, because of the impact of the defense on causation. However, they are not totally exculpatory in most instances because the actor usually has some ability to control whether he does or does not do the unjust harmful act. The fact that there exist so many other people who are subject to the same influences but who effectively choose not to engage in harmful actions is sufficient evidence to determine that full exculpation is unwarranted.

Another type of defense raises issues of mistakes which might have been made, such as "I was aiming at a different target but missed and hit the wrong person," and "I thought he really deserved it because he had hurt her but I was mistaken—he really did not hurt her at all." If we are convinced that bona fide mistakes were involved, then we sometimes ascribe a lesser degree of responsibility to the agent for the act.

The defenses commonly offered regarding the element of the lack of justness are usually arguments of self-defense ("I only did it because I felt threatened") or about means and ends ("I did the harmful act for a higher cause, and therefore I am not blameworthy when the bigger picture is taken into consideration"). While they may have some weight in the mitigation of culpability, particularly if the question of the lack of justness appears to be a close one, these arguments must also have failed in some way the first time around, or else we would not have initially concluded that the act was unjust (which must be the case whenever we reach a mitigation argument).[2]

Because defenses can sometimes affect the assessment of the degree of wrongfulness for any of the elements, they do need to be taken into account before any conclusions are drawn.

Once we have made our determinations about how wrong a given act was with respect to each of the three elements of evil, we can arrive at an overall evaluation of the degree of the immorality entailed in it. Once again, we do this by a balancing process that weighs the conclusions that we have drawn (about the degree of the harm, the degree of responsibility, and the degree of the lack of justness). With each effort of this sort, an immoral act can be located

---

2. The process of adjudicating a case can become more complicated when the wrongdoer essentially has the opportunity to argue for a second time whether the act engaged in was or was not just. However, whether there were close questions on this in the first place will be a primary factor in determining whether raising it again would be appropriate in the context of the assessment of the degree of wrongfulness to assign to the action.

somewhere toward the negative end of the continuum of ethical judgments, from the barely immoral ones down to the basest ones.

The two factors that will move an immoral action toward the bottom end of this scale are: (1) the degree of severity relative to the separate findings concerning each of the three elements, and (2) how those findings are interrelated. The first of these factors recognizes, for example, that there are different degrees of harms: some are relatively minor, and some are horrible. When the latter is the case, it is likely that the act was wrong to a greater degree (and hence that more culpability will be assigned to the agent) than when the harm was minor. An immoral act that causes a death will be more likely to be deemed evil than one that causes a slight bruise, if all other factors were the same. Similarly, different degrees of responsibility correlate with the different types of culpability (intentional harm, harm that derives from a character defect, and negligent harm). The highest degree of culpability attaches to intentionally harmful acts and the lowest degree attaches to those in which neither the act nor the harm was intended but rather were caused by negligence. Intermediate degrees of culpability are usually assigned in cases in which responsibility for the harmful act was due to a reflexive action based in a character-defect. Finally, there are different degrees of unjustness. It is one thing if the victim of an automobile wreck is an innocent child who was required to go along on that fateful journey; it is quite another thing if the injured person is a man who hijacked the car before the accident occurred.

The second factor in an overall assessment of culpability is how the three different assessments we will have made prove to be interrelated. Of course, when all of them are at the negative end of their respective scales, we have identified the most atrocious actions—those which are evil per se. Conversely, when all three are at the opposite end of the spectrums, we have identified one of the "least evils." But those actions which can be placed in the area between the two extremes require more careful reflection if we are to assess culpability accurately.

For purposes of the illustration of how we can and do analyze an action in terms of each of its elements and arrive at our overall conclusions, it may help to consider each of the three elements in two variable positions. One will represent a high degree of that element and the other a low degree (even though, of course, such gradations are not so limited in real life). Within the element of harm, for example, we may think of "low" as a bruise and "high" as an injury resulting in death. For responsibility, "low" might be, for example, a negligent driver whose car suddenly developed bad brakes, and "high" might be a meanspirited action, intentionally carried out. And for the lack of justness element, "low" might be an act which involved a close question about excessive harm caused in self-defense, and "high" might be a cruel and sadistic injury inflicted on another.

Other than when the degrees in the three elements are either all high or all low, none of the other eight combinations which result when these two variables are applied within each of the three categories[3] seems to be correlated directly with any specific location(s) on the general immorality continuum. We simply have no direct one-to-one correlations between any high or low degree in any one of the three elements and final assessments of the overall degree of immorality of wrong actions. We cannot say, for example, that only something caused by intentional harm warrants being described as "evil," because sometimes negligence will suffice. Consider the case of a person who has a major responsibility for the safety of many people—a nuclear engineer in a power plant, for instance, who along with his fellow partygoers falls asleep because they stayed out too late the night before, and whose combined inattentiveness leads to a meltdown and to massive death and disease. When such negligence leads to major catastrophes, the moral judgment which we reach concerning the culpability of the agent should and will be among the most severe. And the same thing holds true for each of the other two elements, as well; a high or a low degree in either of them does not necessarily lead, by itself, to a high or low final assessment of the degree of immorality of a given wrongful act.

---

3. The eight combinations begin with "High harm, high responsibility and high unjustness" and progress through the six intermediate combinations (e.g., "High harm, high responsibility and low unjustness") down to "Low harm, low responsibility and low unjustness."

However, correlations with a more general range of assessments do appear to exist when two of the elements are found to be either in a high or low position. Regardless of which elements we find to be high or low, when any two of them are high and the other one is low, or when any two of them are low and the other one is high, the ranges within which they fall across the immorality spectrum seem to be fairly comparable. When two of them are high and one is low, the immorality valuations lie on the lower side of the spectrum; while when two of them are low and one is high, the ranges extend toward the upper side.

The fact that there appears to be no direct one-to-one correlation between the degree of severity in any single element and the overall degree of immorality that we ascribe to an action, combined with the fact that there does not appear to be any distinction between immorality ranges involving the different elements when any two of them are both high or low, leads me to conclude that the three different elements are of relatively equal importance in determining overall culpability.

An alternative and potentially more precise approach to this process of analysis exists if we can establish a more refined gradation within the categories of harm, responsibility and lack of justness. For example, we could say that the harm done to a victim should be measured in tenths, so that the most atrocious harm would be represented by 1.0 on the scale, and the least by 0.1. Then, if we then were willing to weight all three elements equally,[4] the cumulative value of the worst evil would be 3.0 (1.0 for the highest degree of harm, plus 1.0 for the greatest degree of responsibility, plus 1.0 for the greatest degree of lack of justness). For the least (i.e., most minimally) wrong action, the cumulative value would be 0.3 (0.1 for the least of each of the three elements). All other combinations would be somewhere in between those two extremes (e.g., 1.0 (H)

---

4. We could also weight them differently and still accomplish the same type of general arithmetic valuations if the different relative weights were recognized (e.g., if the degree of moral responsibility is twice as important as the degree of harm when determining the degree of immorality, then the former could have a scale to 2.0).

+ 0.8 (R) + .2 (LJ) = 2.0; 0.4 (H) + 0.2 (R) + 0.6 (LJ) = 1.2; and so on).

The advantage to using such a numerically-based approach would be that it could facilitate the comparison of various actions and thereby lead to productive discussions about their respective moral values. The disadvantage is that it implies that we possess a degree of objectivity that seems, as most ventures into ethical theory show, to be unattainable. The conclusions we draw in making these determinations will always be somewhat inexact because we are dealing with not one but three continuums on which precise value determinations and assignments are often quite difficult. The degree of harm that may be inflicted on someone in any given situation, for example, is not either "horrible" or "negligible"; rather, it may fall at some intermediate point between the two, and collective agreement on exactly where this point may be often is difficult to attain. The same is true for any evaluation in the intermediate ranges of the continuums of the other two elements. But in spite of the fact that such limitations exist, I would propose that this kind of approach could be useful in our comparative evaluations of problematic moral actions.

Thus, the analysis of comparative valuations of immorality is by no means a pure science, but rather a sort of blend between science and art. As Aristotle noted in *Nichomachean Ethics*, we must be content in this area with truth "roughly and in outline."[5] That is, once again, why we need people who have both wisdom and sensitivity to human issues and problems administering our collective systems of justice. Nevertheless, we should be able to fairly ascribe every act of unjust harm to a certain range of immorality if we carefully consider the degrees of each of the three elements and how they fit together.

The degree of immorality that we assign to any given wrongful action has significant consequences. It most directly affects our reactions to the evildoer in question; and that affects, in turn, not

---

5. *The Complete Works of Aristotle*, Jonathan Barnes, ed., Princeton University Press (1984), vol. 2, p. 1730 (Book 1, 3).

only the types of punishment we impose, but also any potential shifts in our assessments of the evildoer's character. In addition, it may affect the victim and his or her family and friends: the greater the magnitude of the wrong, the more that may be demanded by way of sanctions against the evildoer in order that justice be served. If the victim or members of the victim's primary social group believe that the action was such that it created a sort of negative "balance" for the wrongdoer (i.e., some harm that seems to be "due" to him or her), and that for some reason or another this balance has not been cleared, then the possibility also exists that a series of score-evening acts of vengeance will ensue. Furthermore, ascribing the appropriate degree of immorality which attaches to some problematic action is important for the development and maintenance of social norms and standards, since they must be logically coherent and generally applicable. Finally, determining the degree of immorality that is involved is important because these valuations directly affect the ease with which forgiveness may be given. It is, of course, much easier to forgive a slightly immoral act than an egregiously evil one.

While the type and severity of sanctions to be imposed on a wrongdoer will be based primarily upon the degree of immorality that has been ascribed to him, decisions about punishment and reparations are also influenced by other considerations. These can range from certain arguments offered in an attempt to mitigate the wrong to making a special example of some wrongdoer in our efforts to deter others from engaging in additional harmful actions. What one is "due" may thus be, to some extent, a function of the larger moral context in which the particular wrong action was done. We sometimes attempt to diminish the negative consequences to a harmdoer because of actions undertaken after the injury was inflicted (e.g., the perpetrator's personal acknowledgment of guilt, expressions of genuine remorse, attempts at making reparations, or improvements in behavior since the problematic incident). Repentance and reformation arguments do not, of course, directly address the question of culpability, nor do they aid in establishing the degree of the immorality, but rather they can be brought to bear in the determination of appropriate punishment. Another relevant factor is that many of the things that we do have not only direct and intended consequences, but also indirect and unintended ones. If the harmful act under review proves to have set into motion a sequence of further negative actions, or if it inspired others to engage in harmful or destructive behavior, then our assessment of it could be still more adverse, as could our responses to it. On the other hand, a contrary to Murphy's Law might apply, also; for sometimes things that can go right will go right, regardless of our malevolent intentions. If, as a consequence of someone's doing something bad, good things happen, that fact may also affect both our evaluation of and our response to a given immoral action (along the lines of "All's well that ends well").

In order to recognize evil and substantiate our characterization of an act as "evil," we need to understand how to make basic moral decisions and the relevant underlying factual determinations. Even if we find that all three of the elements of evil are present, however, it is still necessary to determine their intensity and severity, and then to assess them collectively, in order to properly assess the degree of immorality which attaches to the action. The result should be a well-reasoned, context-appropriate, and justified assessment of the act in question.

PART II

❧❧

CONFRONTING EVIL AND OTHER
FORMS OF IMMORALITY

6

AVOIDING PERSONAL IMMORALITY

However we characterize the moral nature of man—whether we believe that men and women are basically good, basically bad, or basically neither—we must integrate into that world view the fact that evil and other manifestations of immorality are pervasive in our lives. Few innocent lives are untouched by evil very long; and still fewer are the number of mature individuals who have not, in one way or another, indulged in, stooped to, or otherwise participated in evil-doing or other forms of immorality, at least on an occasional basis. The "gains" to be had from acting immorally, whether large or small, are too tempting for most of us to resist completely, particularly if we happen to begin from morally weak or compromised positions (resulting from troublesome early relationships, poor or nonexistent moral training, etc.). Indeed, some people argue fairly convincingly that evil is natural because it furthers evolutionary demands. Citing animal as well as human behavior, Lyall Watson argued, in *Dark Nature: A Natural History of Evil*,[1] that we are naturally and genetically guided by the following three rules: (1) be nasty to outsiders; (2) be nice to insiders; and (3) cheat whenever

---

1. Harper Collins (New York, 1995), pp. 54-65.

possible.[2] According to Watson, when individuals do these things, their offspring and other close kin are more likely to survive; and when they do not, their offspring and kin are more likely to perish. Regardless of what the reasons may be, however, from genetic programming to malevolent free choice, the fact is that most of us do at least some things that are not morally right from time to time. And the fact is that all of us are capable of doing wrong anew almost every day, because opportunities to make moral or immoral decisions regularly confront us.

Because almost all of us ethically err at least occasionally, the main question concerning avoidance of personal immorality is perhaps better put initially in terms of how we can successfully deal with any given opportunity that we may have to do something wrong, rather than in terms of how we might manage its "permanent" avoidance. Journeys are, after all, made up of individual steps. In addition, any sustained effort at avoiding of *all* immorality would, for most of us, have to be conditioned on something other than a full—or, indeed, a "normal"—life. To lead a virtually immorality-free life (or even something closely resembling it), one would probably have to withdraw from our complex day-to-day world, in which competing ethical interests and diverse moral relationships and duties can make it difficult to avoid making at least occasional moral mistakes—even if we regularly desire to do the right thing. Hence, some men and women seeking to live moral lives withdraw into the isolation of deserts and forests or band together into small communities of ethically-homogeneous thinkers (e.g., in monasteries and convents). But even for the ascetic, complete moral purity is likely difficult to achieve, because certain vices would continue to be temptations (such as excessive pride or covetousness). Attempts to attain complete moral perfection under normal living circumstance can lead to repetitive and discouraging failures. Therefore, for the majority of us, it is probably more helpful to know how to minimize our moral errors in the course of everyday life.

---

2. Of course, being nice to insiders is both a benevolence and a fidelity duty, so one of these "rules" is a matter of ethical, rather than unethical, behavior.

The first part of this chapter discusses why we should want to avoid personal immorality, while the second offers suggestions as to how to do that, particularly when we are otherwise tempted.

Reasons for Not Acting Immorally

As with most endeavors that are subject to our intentions, the major variable in our success in choosing not to act immorally is our motivation. If we are capable of doing something, then whether or not we do it depends first upon whether we want to; if we *want* to avoid some evil or otherwise immoral action, then we usually *can*. On the other hand, if we are not particularly motivated to do so, we may have substantial difficulties. If we are not actively trying to avoid performing certain actions, then whether we succeed in avoiding them depends largely on luck or on intervention by others, and neither of those can protect us from doing wrong things on a regular basis.

This does not mean that the effort we need to make in order to avoid doing wrong is necessarily always a strenuous one. Despite Lyall Watson's observations about the naturalness of immoral behavior, we human beings also appear to have some innate ethical tendencies; and we may even have a biological impetus toward certain types of moral behavior. James Q. Wilson, for example, argues in *The Moral Sense* that good is natural.[3] Regardless of how we start out, however, or why we start out the way we do, when we reach an age at which we become morally responsible for our actions, our choices are, to a significant extent, under our own control. If we want to be motivated to do certain things, there are steps that we can take to cultivate that motivation-to help it grow in strength and thus to crowd out competing motivations.

An important step in this process of cultivating proper motivation is understanding the various reasons why we should or should not do the things that we might be considering doing. If we convince ourselves that it makes sense to want to do something (or not do it)—that, for example, it is reasonable in some way to avoid or

---

3. The Free Press (New York, 1993).

suppress an impulse to hurt someone—then we usually try to direct our intentional behavior accordingly. As rational beings, we often *do* respond fairly well to the justificatory arguments of reason.

Several different types of reasons help explain why we should try to resist the opportunities that we have to do something that is immoral. Generally speaking, these include the following five categories: philosophical, psychological, social, religious and practical.

The primary philosophical reason to avoid doing evil is derived from our most basic and general moral duty, which is the duty to be ethical. In order to achieve this—both in specific circumstances and with respect to our overall moral characters—we have to consistently try to do the right thing. If we really want to achieve something, we cannot regularly engage in action to the contrary at the same time. Because we have an ethical duty to try to do what is right, part of performing that duty—particularly when we are dealing with things that may lead us down the negative side of the ethical continuum—is *trying not* to do what is wrong (which could be called our general affirmative avoidance duty). In other words, if we accept the proposition that as potentially ethical beings we should try to be ethical, we should not simultaneously try to do things that are wrong.

Even if we do not agree that we have the moral duty to try to become as ethical as we possibly can (and, indeed, many have problems with this proposition to one degree or another, as a general conclusion or as a premise for our daily lives), most of us would at least be willing to concede that we should have the moral objective of trying not to be unethical, which translates into the goal of trying to keep ourselves at least somewhere in the middle of the morality continuum. Although few of us seem to be striving for sainthood, most of us also have no overriding interest in becoming demons. But even if our objective is only to occupy what we might term the moral middle ground, we still have to try—at least most of the time—to avoid wrong actions.[4]

---

4. If half of a person's moral decisions are right and half are wrong, that individual would be found well toward the low end of the Bell Curve of the human moral continuum. It does not take a high percentage of wrong choices to be deemed morally troublesome.

More specific philosophical reasons that can motivate us to avoid immoral actions are related to the different general approaches that we take in determining what is ethical. Our moral guidance for dealing with issues involving pleasure and pain, for example, leads us to act with restraint and to moderate our efforts to obtain personal pleasure and avoid personal pain. To do otherwise is to engage in excess, in one direction or another. Indulgence in excess leads to unpleasant and inappropriate consequences not only for the agent but also for others who are indirectly affected by it. While the unrestrained pursuit of excess often appears to have numerous proponents, its rejection as a moral principle has been almost universally endorsed. Understanding the consequences of excess makes us disposed to follow a path of moderation in issues involving the pursuit of pleasure and the avoidance of pain, and thus helps us be motivated to avoid immoral actions that emanate from the extremes of this spectrum.

When we take an ethical approach to matters involving self-realization, doing what is ethical means seeking one's own personal growth and self-fulfillment, and doing what is unethical means failing to do those things. Various methods and degrees of self-abnegation or self-destruction have been proposed by nihilists, by pessimists, and by those who believe that it is necessary to abandon the ideal of self-realization in any worldly context in order to achieve some even greater value (usually involving the next world). But the nihilists are fundamentally and logically wrong, for not only their arguments but also their actions turn out to be contradictory in one way or another.[5] Pessimists cannot ultimately succeed in devaluing the hope of achieving present moral worth through self-development. And many of those who see the individual or the ego as "the problem" also see its development in *their* favored direction as a laudable—or even necessary—goal (in other words, self-realization for them is extolled when it is called by another name and sought via a somewhat different path).[6] To either consciously move or allow oneself to be

---

5. For example, nihilism provides its own "ought's" even when it denies their general validity.
6. Most "dropouts" still seek something or some things, even if it is their stated goal is not to seek "things" (by which they mainly mean

moved toward personal despair and disintegration is thus appropriately considered to be morally wrong (regardless of our current
degree of moral angst). If we understand the moral principles which
underlie our search for self-realization, then we should become more
motivated to refuse to succumb to actions that lead away from this
goal.

Another ethical approach is fidelity, which encompasses both
loyalty and honesty. If we are loyal to the individuals to whom we
have special duties (e.g., to our children or employers), to those
social groups to which we have the obligation of fealty (e.g., our
communities or countries), and to God, we must try to avoid
breaches of those obligations. We thus need to try to keep from
doing wrong things in the context of our relationships of primary
import. We are not being good relatives if we hurt someone in our
immediate family, nor are we being good group members if we resist
the implementation of an important legitimate policy by that group.
Those of us who are Christians or Jews are not being loyal to God
if we violate the Decalogue. And, generally speaking, we should
adhere to our word and try to avoid dishonesty. As we better
understand the fidelity approach—as it begins to make more sense
to us why its goals are moral and why disloyalty and dishonesty are
immoral—we should feel an increasingly greater inclination to make
the effort to avoid such actions.

The principle of benevolence is composed of several duties,
ranged as follows: (1) the duty to avoid harming others; (2) the duty
to avoid doing injustice to others; (3) the duty to do justice to others;
and (4) at least sometimes, the duty to be charitable to others. On
this approach, we do what is unethical if we cause unjust harm or
otherwise do injustice to other people. However, we can also be
unethical if we avoid doing justice, or if we fail to do at least some
charity. While some philosophers (e.g., Nietzsche) have derided our
benevolence obligations in favor of the pursuit of other ethical
objectives (first and foremost, self-realization), benevolence is one
of our legitimate major approaches to the ethical. It also provides us

---

the things, tangible and intangible, that most other people seek, but
not the new things, tangible or intangible, that they have decided to
seek for themselves.)

with specific philosophical reasons for avoiding doing things that are immoral in this context. As we better understand what is moral and what is not with respect to these obligations, we should become more motivated not only to avoid causing unjust harm or committing acts of injustice, but also not to fail to act justly and charitably.

In addition to philosophical reasons for not acting immorally, psychological reasons support such efforts. Psychology also helps us understand why we are sometimes motivated to choose a direction which is diametrically opposed to the moral and the good.

At times we are strongly attracted to evil and other forms of immorality—even in the abstract. Particularly when we are young and just learning about life, curiosity and excitement can precipitate a deliberate moral transgression, which is often followed by fright, and then either delight or chagrin. This phenomenon is associated with the development of personal independence and autonomy and with relatively normal forms of rebellion against parents and other authorities. The thrill that can come from "getting away with it" through a breach of moral expectations is perhaps based in the allure of transgressing a certain defined limit on social behavior. We may try to justify such an action in terms of a desire to "experience" that side of life, too, even if (or sometimes perhaps even because) we have been well trained to want to be ethical. Such a psychologically-based impetus to engage in evil and other forms of immorality can be fairly common, and it is not abnormal to be drawn to it. But when we begin to understand that these transgressions often bring only relatively small emotional pleasures—what we might term a "fleeting thrill"—it may become easier for us to resist doing the wrong merely to satisfy that itch.

Psychology can also help us identify, understand and deal with some of our darker, emotionally-based urges before they lead us into ethical trouble. We are all aware, for example, that outbursts triggered by anger can lead us to hurt others, and that when such an action is unjustified, it is wrong. The knowledge that anger can and often does lead us to do things which subsequent moral reflection will condemn creates for us a moral obligation to try to control our anger. In other words, an understanding of the psychology of the emotions can help us in our struggle to control them.

The problems associated with certain mental disorders constitutes another type of psychological reason for avoiding doing morally wrong things. All of us have at least some degree of moral sensibility; and, consequently, doing something which is genuinely evil or engaging in some other sort of immoral action can create guilt, anxiety and depression.[7] It can also lead to self-contempt or self-loathing (as opposed to psychologically sound self-love). These paths are associated with a number of psychological disorders, from certain neuroses to clinical depression to sociopathology. It is, therefore, in the interest of our overall psychological health and well-being to try, wherever possible, to avoid doing things that are wrong.

We may, however, need to watch the degree of our efforts here, because they could become counterproductive, to some extent. Carl Jung, for example, believed that we will always have a darker side (which he called the "shadow"), and that we try to vanquish all evil within us at our peril. In fact, he thought that if we try to eliminate the dark side completely, it simply develops into something even more evil and destructive. He wrote, "The fact is that if one tries beyond one's capacity to be perfect, the Shadow descends to hell and becomes the devil. For it is just as sinful from the standpoint of nature and of truth to be above oneself as to be below oneself."[8]

There are also several major social reasons for avoiding evil and other forms of immorality. Many of our important groups have advanced their causes by the ethical actions of their members—in particular, when they collectively fulfill their loyalty duties. Various groups, from our nations to our companies, schools, unions, and social clubs, also benefit from having citizens, students, teachers and other types of members who generally lead ethically balanced lives—people who do not regularly seek excessive pleasure, who try to become self-realized, and who try to avoid unjustly hurting others

---

7. For example, criminals whose primary ethics is found within their small group loyalties would feel badly about breaking those bonds.
8. *The Vision Seminars*, Spring, Zurich, 1976, as quoted in Watson (247-248). Jung also wrote: "The best is the most threatened with some devilish perversion just because it has done the most to suppress evil." *Symbols of Transformation*, Routledge Kegan Paul (London and Henley, 1981), p. 375.

or causing injustice to them, and so on. Groups with higher percentages of members who act ethically (and who also try to avoid acting unethically) are generally more cohesive and therefore stronger—particularly over the long term—than groups with smaller percentages of members who act ethically (and who also try to avoid acting unethically). From this we can conclude that such groups do benefit when we try to avoid unethical behavior; and to the extent that we are loyal to them, we will try to do that.

By contrast, our groups tend to be diminished, and they can actually be harmed, when we do not try to avoid unethical behavior, since it breaks the loyalty and benevolence bonds that help ensure solidarity. The success of a group tends to correlate directly with the effective performance of the reciprocal moral obligations that exist among its members. If unethical behavior of members becomes a widespread problem, or if such behavior becomes too readily tolerated, the group as a whole is weakened. Furthermore, if such behavior predominates, the group itself can become dysfunctional and may, at some point, even dissolve. Another valid reason for avoiding personal immorality is therefore to help insure the survival and growth of such essential groups.

A more immediate and direct social reason to abstain from unethical behavior is provided by and through the deterrents of our legal systems. Every government establishes laws, and these laws impose a comprehensive framework for and limits on individual and subgroup behavior based upon some of the group's collective moral beliefs. Laws are a subset of ethical rules. They are established by governments to obtain behavioral conformity to what the leaders have established as some of the main rules of right and wrong within a given political system. Many individual laws coincide with the moral positions of a substantial portion of the group, as interpreted by the group's leaders. Violation of a law therefore breaches not only our ethical duty of group loyalty, but it also constitutes a challenge to collectively drawn conclusions about the morality of the specific act in question. Furthermore, while our major social groups usually make illegal only the most serious types of moral transgressions (e.g., murder, theft, etc.), most legal systems also allow civil recourse for intentional or negligent injuries caused to others. Thus, another significant social reason to avoid evil and other forms of immorality is that our actions very well may be actionable; and if so, then additional sanctions for violating the rights of others may be imposed on us (such as monetary damages awarded to the victim) if we do not avoid the commission of such offenses. Knowing that there is a personal risk of being subject to formal punishment or being ordered to pay monetary damages should normally help motivate us to want not to do a wrong when that action would also constitute the breaking of a law and/or the violation of the legal rights of others.

Religions provide yet another set of reasons why we should want to avoid immoral actions. In addition to the fact that religious institutions are also social groups and would therefore impose on us the same types of obligations and restrictions discussed above, religions provide a basis for the aspirations of its members for continued existence in some form or another after death. Christians and Muslims aspire to reach heaven, Hindus and Buddhists seek to be reborn to a better life, Buddhists also endeavor to attain nonexistence, and so forth. All of these seem to be contingent, at least to some degree, upon leading ethical lives (as interpreted by the precepts of that religion), and thus upon avoiding doing evil and other forms of immorality. Hence, if we want our souls to benefit in the next life, we should conform to religious directives to be good and to eschew evil.

Finally, there are also some important practical reasons to want to avoid doing evil, given some of the consequences that seem to follow from it. The first of these is the tendency of evil to implode. Repeatedly engaging in wrong actions is a behavioral pattern that is not sustainable, either individually or corporately; such action is essentially self-destructive in nature. This happens most often because the evildoers become dissolute, reckless or suicidal; but it also occurs because evildoers tend to generate and attract active opposition from others, who will seek to protect themselves from the dangers they perceive to be threatening them. The implosion of evil is simply a consequence of the fact that it resides on the negative ground of being.

A second practical reason for avoiding evil is that the negative ground of being (which is the natural locus of evil) is simply not a place where we, as human beings, want to remain. If we do, we will find that its denizens are all those things that we normally seek to avoid—unhappiness, death, dissatisfaction, failure, suffering, and the many related conditions that we do not normally want either to be subject to or to be in the presence of. Absent some type of mental disorientation, we generally desire to be in the positive ground of being—at least when we are rational—so that we can share, as much as possible, in the conditions that have been identified with a good life, including such things as happiness, satisfaction, success and social approbation, and their related rewards.

Consideration of these five types of reasons for avoiding evil—the philosophical, the psychological, the social, the religious and the practical—can help us to avoid evil, but motivating ourselves to do so is by no means a purely rational exercise. We are motivated by many things other than reason or the prospect of acting reasonably. Indeed, our motivations usually reflect to a significant extent our emotions and desires; the primary impetus for wanting something or for wanting to do something is often emotional. But even our emotions are, to some extent, malleable. We can, with regular effort and "exercise," control those which are negative—anger and fear, for example; and thereafter we can avoid engaging in some wrong actions. Through self-discipline, self-control, and personal conditioning . . . by repeatedly strengthening our abilities to contain and restrain our impulses, we can make these things moral habits.

The training we receive from others is another major way in which we can strengthen the motivation to avoid doing what is unethical. Such training comes to us from various sources, the most important ones being our parents and other close family members, teachers and religious leaders, mentors, friends and close associates. It includes both direct and indirect motivational assistance. We learn early on that we need to avoid doing wrong in order to avoid the displeasure and sanctions of those who are close to us and of others who may have powers over us in one way or another. This training is not merely passively received, either, for we often seek out such assistance from others. Most of us frequently ask the advice of family and friends on many different kinds of moral questions; and if we have significant or persistent problems, we can also seek the help of professional counselors. Other people often know more than we do about specific moral questions; and therefore their information, their more "objective" vantage points on specific actions, and their encouragement to right action can be of great assistance. Their insights can strengthen our resolve to avoid specific wrongs when we are presented with the opportunities to do so.

Unless we possess a strong motivation to avoid unethical actions, we cannot possibly be successful at it. Unnecessary immoral and evil acts are almost certain to follow from the carelessness or bad character traits that tend to grow within a moral vacuum. Working on having a good character—or at least, one which is not bad—is an ongoing prerequisite to actually having one. And we must want to have a good (or a not-bad) character before we can make any serious effort toward developing (or retaining) one.

Tactics for Avoiding Immorality

While motivation may be a necessary precondition for any sustained effort at avoiding immoral action, good intentions alone hardly suffice. Additional steps must be taken if we are to avoid wrongdoing. These steps include developing and refining our skills in the following areas: identifying unethical or potentially unethical actions; understanding why we may be tempted to do wrong; confronting our personal inclinations to do specific wrongs; being willing to seek help from others when we are being tempted; having the foresight to avoid or minimize temptations; having the strength to cease our involvement in an immoral activity before its conclusion, if we have been participating in it; and, finally, having the humility and resolve to learn from our ethical mistakes. I will address each of these areas in turn.

If we do not have the ability to identify specific opportunities for doing wrong things as they occur, we will not be good at avoiding them. Even if we are generally motivated both to do the right thing and not to do the wrong thing, we can still stumble into engaging in wrong actions through ignorance and error; but some of these mistakes would be preventable, and neither ignorance nor error would excuse them. In other words, if, with increased dedication, effort or understanding on our part (all of which are within our control), we would not have been ignorant or mistaken in a way that led to an unjust harmful act, we will be judged culpable for that act. It is therefore imperative that we develop, expand and refine our powers of moral discernment. We need to be able to identify and correctly categorize specific actions, activities and situations that are likely to have immoral consequences.

The ability to identify an action as immoral in advance of engaging in it—either in the immediate future or at some more distant point in time—requires a basic understanding of ethical principles. At the very least, we need to know which things are clearly right and which clearly wrong. This should not pose much of a problem, because there is rarely any confusion about the nature of actions which lie at both ends of the morality continuum (even though the grey areas may be troublesome). It also helps us (particularly for purposes of strengthening our personal motivation) to understand why some things are wrong.

Once we have begun to become skillful at recognizing potentially unethical actions, we need to apply that ability to situations as they present themselves to us. Requisite to this is a minimal facility with logic. Logic provides us with the capability of deducing from an understanding and acceptance of the proposition that hurting others is ordinarily wrong, and from the knowledge that cutting the person in front of me (as with a sharp instrument) would hurt him, the conclusion that it would be wrong to do so (absent, of course, extenuating circumstances, such as if I were a surgeon operating on that person with his informed consent). It is in this very direct fashion that we first learn (and teach) how to use ethical principles. As children, we imbibed basic ethical principles and were told how and when to apply them. We subsequently pass on the same basic moral guidance to our own children in the hope that they will lead morally acceptable lives.

Correctly identifying a wrong ethical path can sometimes be as difficult as identifying a right one, given the various approaches we take to the resolution of moral issues, and given the level of complexity we are sometimes faced with in everyday life. But this merely means that we have to be willing to work a little harder at discerning what would be wrong in a specific situation, so as to know precisely what it is that we need to avoid.

Once we have determined that an action which we are contemplating is potentially immoral, if we do not immediately turn away from it, we will need to directly confront any desire that we may have to go ahead and do it anyway. Wrong not only has its own psychological allure, as noted above, but it also can sometimes bring us certain "rewards"—things that we want that appear to us to be personal gains (particularly in the short term). We all need certain material goods to sustain ourselves. Most of us desire more of them than we have at any given point in time; and thieves, for example, manage to obtain more (if they are "successful"). Indeed, most immoral acts are done with the expectation of gaining some perceived personal advantage of one type or another. Understanding our motivations is therefore key to successfully facing down the temptation to do something unethical.

Along these lines, we need to remind ourselves that as human beings, we are subject to diverse (and sometimes divergent) wants and urges, that not infrequently we react emotionally when a more rational response is demanded, and that almost all of us probably have at least some immoral thoughts and desires at one time or another. The fact that we may sometimes want to do something wrong therefore should not be frightening to us or seem unusual; it is a fact of life, and recognizing that fact can help us move forward in dealing with it. In other words, conceding that from time to time we really want to do something wrong, even though we are generally inclined to do what is right, we should be more effective in trying to control those motivations if we are able to identify them. Knowing exactly why we may want to do what is wrong in a specific situation allows us to focus on that motivating desire. We can isolate it, see its long-term limitations, its inadequacies, and all of its potentially negative consequences, and then we can deal with it more efficaciously. And doing so is very important, especially in the case of recurrent evil thoughts; because if evil thoughts are suffered frequently or for long periods, the chances of their fruition grow. As the Buddha is quoted as saying in *The Dhammapada*,[9] "Suffering follows an evil thought as the wheels of a cart follow the oxen that draw it."

In this connection, the fact that we have desires to do immoral things does not mean that doing them is in any way ethically

---

9. Trans. Eknath Easwaran, Nilgiri Press (Petaluma, California, 1986), p. 78.

legitimate, even though we are sometimes quite convinced by our attempted rationalizations along these lines. With enough effort, we can usually direct our minds properly, just as we can our bodies.

Effective responses to evil thoughts can take a variety of forms. We can repress them, rationally confront them, divert them, or force ourselves to move on beyond them. We can list reasons for abandoning such thoughts. We can substitute other, more positive thoughts for them. We can give vent to evil ideas in relatively harmless ways (e.g., write a nasty letter to someone who has angered us, but then burn it). And we can try to work out alternative responses to them and try to strengthen those. In short, when dealing with impulses to do wrong, we can stifle them, argue with them, fake them out, ignore them, or turn our attention to something else. We have the ability to move them along by one means or another and push them out of our consciousness.

Identifying wrong actions in which we might engage and trying to overcome any desire we may have to move in those directions only begins to address the problem. We still have to fulfill our moral duty not to make choices that would lead to unethical actions. The moral imperative that normally applies at the moment of decision-making is "just don't do it." However, there are also some last-minute tactics that can help move us in the right direction. If we need to promise ourselves a personal reward for not doing something wrong, that would usually be acceptable, if it produces the desired results. If we need to threaten ourselves with some sort of personal punishment should we succumb to the desire to engage in some immoral action and that threat would help deter us from it, that would usually be fine, as well, if it would assist in preventing us from doing it. We can legitimately and effectively employ our own rewards and punishments in order to help us move in the right directions.

There are, however, cases in which our own personal efforts prove insufficient to resist the temptation to do something unethical, and in such situations we should seek the assistance of others. Many people are ready, willing and able to help us avoid evil and other forms of immorality. All we have to do is access their insights or resources, or at least be receptive to them. Personal counseling often works, to one degree or another. Collective efforts to help individuals resist the temptation to do the wrong thing can also be successful, as in the case of Alcoholics Anonymous. Participating in small groups whose primary intentions are to do good things, such as religious groups (through churches, temples, mosques, and so on), service groups (e.g., Rotary or Lions Clubs), or recreation and development groups (like the YMCA or Boys and Girls Clubs), can also provide opportunities for social interaction that lead us both toward doing positive things and also away from doing negative ones.

In addition to understanding how to deal with temptations which are immediately before us, we also need to try to avoid potential future temptations. Some of these come from within ourselves—from our desires, emotions, needs and wants; but others have eternal causes. We may not have the slightest interest in doing a specific wrong until, voila! the opportunity suddenly presents itself.

Most external temptations do not, however, startle us, because, in fact, we know where many of them are or where many of them are likely to be found. To minimize the times we will end up doing the wrong thing, we can deliberately reduce the number of temptations that we have to face simply by staying away from such places. Some temptations may be found in certain locations (e.g., in a specific bar). Others may be found in certain people who, for one reason or another (usually their own personal gain) want us to do something that is wrong (e.g., drug dealers). Other temptations may be found in specific things, like alcohol for an alcoholic. Once again, a critical element in any effort to minimize unethical activity is simply to avoid those places, people and things that might weaken or undo our resolve to control ourselves—resolve which would be quite sufficient if it were not strongly tested.

If we do not now know about the specific types of temptations that we need to avoid, then it is incumbent upon us to learn about them. This is not to suggest that we have to learn by doing, but rather by regularly seeking to be more knowledgeable about ourselves and the various external sources of temptation that exist. Certain types of knowledge are readily accessible to us. We are aware, for example, of situations that have gotten not only us but also others into trouble before, and we can know or figure out where those situations might exist or be developing. We can also learn more about the people with whom we associate and try to understand where they may try to lead us, and why. We can become more cognizant of specific potential inducements to engage in evil acts, and thereafter appropriately direct ourselves away from them.

Finally, even if we cannot entirely avoid the places, people or things that may tempt us, there are still other ways in which we can deal with specific temptations to do wrong. We can focus all of our strength and efforts on resisting them, or we can move ourselves in the direction of less tempting places, people and things. We can also remain on special alert for the typical indicators of specific temptations—the overt and covert inducements that are presented to us together with their accompanying rationalizations (which frequently rely on invalid means/ends arguments). If all else fails, we can try to divert our energies into doing the less harmful of several potential wrongs. (Lesser evils are, after all, lesser.)

This chapter has thus far focused mainly on how we can avoid doing wrong ourselves. The last part of it, however, will deal with the question of how to avoid doing still more or greater wrongs in circumstances in which we have already become, for one reason or another, involved in an immoral activity. If I am the only one doing something wrong, the matter is straightforward: I can simply stop doing it. But if I am caught up (intentionally or otherwise) in some evil enterprise in which others are also engaged in wrongdoing, the problems that can occur when I try to exit from it can be substantially more complicated. Sometimes it may be as simple as saying, "I quit," but doing this can be extremely difficult if the others do not want to stop and also do not want you to stop. Other people can provide strong negative inducements for us to continue along the same path (e.g., blackmail, threats of physical violence, or bribes). Even some people who have not been participating directly may react negatively to a proposal by someone to withdraw from a wrongful activity. This would, of course, include those who may be benefitting from it indirectly even without participating in it, and those who have accepted an invalid means/end argument offered in support of such actions. In addition, a person who withdraws from wrongful activity can face not only exposure to legitimate punishment, but also inappropriately damaging consequences (e.g., threats from someone in authority who wishes to exact excessive punishment). Thus, the personal costs of exiting from an immoral enterprise can be high, and sometimes even egregious.

But upon discovering that we are involved in an unethical enterprise, or upon realizing that we finally have just gotten fed up with being a part of one, we are ethically obligated to extract ourselves from it. We should remove ourselves from the collective enterprise as skillfully as possible, with minimum damage to ourselves and others. Needless to say, this often requires that we not only draw on all of our internal moral strength, but also that we make use of any and all other resources that may be available to us.

The final step in a comprehensive effort to avoid personal wrongdoing involves learning from our moral mistakes. Almost all of us make them, and many of us even do some things which, at least in retrospect, could be categorized as evil (or something close to it). One of our best opportunities for learning on the moral level immediately follows the recognition that we have ethically erred. If we are willing to take a hard look at our mistakes and then to take responsibility for them, we will enhance our ability to deter ourselves from repeating them. This is particularly true if we impose appropriate punishment upon ourselves as part of the consequences for the ethical error that we have committed (cf. doing penance). The same is the case if we accept appropriate punishment from others and attempt to make proper reparations for our wrongs. Even though this is not always possible, if we want to be moral and if we slip up, we *should* feel guilty (to some extent), we *should* appropriately suffer for our mistakes (to some extent), and we *should* appropriately atone for them. These are simply the ethical consequences of a part of the duty to act benevolently in these situations—the duty to do justice. We can, of course, go overboard with respect to self-deterrence, just as in many other areas (feeling guilty and continuing to suffer may, for example, become inappropriate and even harmful once we have accepted responsibility for our errors and properly atoned for them). In short, if we truly want to avoid engaging in further wrong or immoral actions to the best of our ability to do so, reacting appropriately after we err is a necessary part of that effort.

◊   ◊   ◊   ◊

To summarize briefly, avoiding personal wrongdoing and other forms of immorality is a continuous enterprise that is rarely completely successful. We may have many good reasons to want to avoid doing the wrong things, but there are also numerous enticements to do them. Fortunately for us, if we want to take the effort to acquire skill in avoiding personal immorality, we can become ever more successful in doing so.

7

OPPOSING EVIL AROUND US

W henever any individual avoids personal immorality as best he or she can, the world is a better place, at least in some small ways. Fewer immoral acts occur than might otherwise be the case, and each life lived morally serves as a positive example to others. While we often recognize that evil spreads (e.g., "One rotten apple can spoil the whole bushel"), good does, too.

If, however, each of us were to work only on our own personal morality, the world would not become the better place it could have become had we expanded our efforts. While we are alive, we have the opportunity to reduce the amount of evil and other forms of immorality that others might do—just as they have the opportunity to do the same with respect to our actions. As noted earlier, ethics is a collective enterprise; and when we ignore chances to have a positive moral impact on others, we do so at some ethical peril and cost.

Of all the dangerous things we may do in this life, however, few may compare to actively opposing evil and other forms of immorality being done by others. In the first place, such activities will almost inevitably anger those whom we are trying to thwart, either because we will become an impediment to their attaining their personal goals or because we will be perceived as evildoers ourselves (because many of them will have been convinced by erroneous means/ends arguments). Active opposition to evil often arouses an equal and opposite reaction, and it can be perilous, both to ourselves and to those who are associated with us. And all of these problems can occur even when we are right! We subject ourselves to significant additional personal risks if we happen to be wrong; for then we will not only face the active opposition of those whom we are trying to thwart, but we will also have to deal with the consequences of making a moral mistake (and perhaps an egregious one). When we take active stands against what we perceive to be immorality, there is often a chance that we could be mistaken about the situation. Consequently, we could find that we have become involved in a moral quagmire of massive proportions if it turns out that what we assumed to be right was, in fact, wrong, and thus that instead of thwarting evil, we have actually damaged someone else's legitimate ethical enterprise. Finally, in addition to all these dangers, there are other "costs": opposing evil and other forms of immorality takes time and consumes energy and resources that could all be put to good use in other endeavors.

This chapter begins by considering why, despite the dangers and costs, we should oppose at least some instances of evil when we encounter it. It then moves on to make some suggestions on how this can be done successfully. It also examines the special choices that victims have in dealing with evil, including the propriety and necessity of forgiveness and mercy, and ends with some conclusions and caveats about our efforts in this area.

Reasons for Opposing Evil Done by Others

So why should we go looking for trouble by intruding into the unethical affairs of others? I propose that we should do so for the same kinds of reasons for which we should avoid personal immorality, namely, for philosophical, psychological, social, religious and practical ones, as cited in a different context in the previous chapter.

The main ethical reason to oppose the evil being done by others is simply because it is our moral responsibility to do so. To do otherwise would violate our benevolence duties to be just and charitable. Evil and other forms of immorality cause unjustified harm to others. We fulfill our obligation to do justice to those who are being (or who may be) unjustifiably harmed if we interfere with the efforts of those who are seeking to cause them such harm.

Another philosophical reason for intervening in a troublesome situation can sometimes be found in our duty to be loyal, under the fidelity approach to the analysis of moral action. We have a special duty to protect others with whom we are involved in relationships of primary import (e.g., family, friends, or students). If they are being threatened with unjust harm from others, we are *supposed* to come to their defense. The same is true for some of our larger groups, like our countries. If one of them is being threatened (especially with such things as military invasions), then as members of the group which is in danger, we have a duty to come to its defense.

Thus, we often need to fulfill our fidelity and benevolence obligations by opposing the potentially immoral acts of others. Indeed, in some of these situations, omitting or neglecting to do so would be immoral. There are clearly times when we must try to deter some impending injury or evil, and, if appropriate, punish those responsible for it.

Psychological reasons for opposing evil being done or threatened by others are both positive and negative. To some extent, our personal development and emotional well-being may depend upon our ability to act courageously when it becomes imperative that we try to prevent some impending wrongdoing. Our psychological adjustment is better if we meet legitimate expectations for morally responsible action in those situations. On the other hand, if we fail to try to stop some evils that may be occurring, we may also suffer certain kinds of continuing psychological harm. A sense of guilt follows upon reflection on personal cowardice. Longer term, such inactions may lead to sustained pain caused by the dissonance that results from recognizing the difference between the person we know ourselves to be in contrast to the person we know we should have become.

There are also social reasons for opposing evil that is being done by others. In every group, social order and progress are dependent, to some extent, upon the degree of immorality being done within the group and the degree being tolerated by it. In the long term, a group can only advance—and, in fact, it may only survive—if it does not suffer excessive immorality within it. Furthermore, extended periods of evil beget oppression, and the social ramifications of internal oppression are highly negative for every group. Loyalty would dictate that, as members of a group, we should try to encourage and contribute to the moral soundness of the group as a whole. Finally, while we rarely have a legal duty to prevent evil (for the criminal laws of most countries do not require this), another social reason to oppose the evil we see happening around us is that civil laws may allow penalties to be imposed for negligent omissions in certain situations (e.g., damages may be awarded against a hotel owner that fails to take reasonable steps to protect its guests from harm).

Religious reasons for opposing evil are presented initially in the words of their founders and their primary texts, and adherents are bound by a duty of loyalty to those teachings. All the world's major religions generally exhort us to do good and oppose the evil that exists in this world. In addition, religions make a connection between opposing evil here and now and aspirations for a positive afterlife. If we want to reach heaven, achieve a better reincarnation, or attain nirvana, we must lead a life that would merit this. To the extent that our actions have an impact on our afterlives, if we fail to prevent evil when we are in a position to do so, our chances of achieving what we hope for in the hereafter would be diminished.

In addition to philosophical, psychological, social and religious reasons for opposing evil, there are also certain practical reasons for doing so. The first such practical reason involves self-defense. Aggressive evil tends to expand unless and until it is stopped. Sooner or later, such evil might reach our shores and our doorsteps. Even though the threat may not be an immediate one, persons committing evil, if they remain unchecked, may at some point want to harm us or those near to us. Opposing evil in the present, before self-defense has become an urgent matter, may therefore simply be a prudent and effective course of action. Such pre-emptive measures often make strategic sense as well, because the likelihood of success is usually greater if we attempt to root out evil earlier rather than later (i.e., before it has gained strength or while there are numerous options for defending against it). As David R. Blumenthal notes in *The Banality of Good and Evil,*[1] "lesser acts prepare the way for more grave acts . . . and routinization facilitates the doing of evil."

Another practical reason for opposing evil is that even our failure in such an effort may still be important. If there is any chance of success whatsoever, it might—at least sometimes—be better to be defeated than to acquiesce to the imposition of evil and to its attendant oppression. Furthermore, even if we cannot successfully resist the particular evil in question, perhaps we can make some sort of inroad into it, or at least inspire others who might follow our lead and be more likely to succeed. As Alfred, Lord Tennyson might have said, is it not better to have fought evil and lost than never to have fought it at all?[2]

We have, therefore, strong philosophical, psychological, social, religious and practical reasons for choosing to oppose evil and other forms of immorality that are presently being done by others or that they are threatening to do. Once we make a decision to oppose it, however, we need determine exactly what we should oppose, because there are so many alternatives that we could not undertake all of them in many lifetimes. Then we need to work out a strategy for conducting an effective campaign against it.

Tactics for Opposing Evil Done by Others

Perhaps the easiest way to oppose evil is as a follower in a group which is on the right track. In such circumstances, we do not have the primary burden of making decisions that will, to a significant extent, lead the group in either a moral or immoral direction. Even followers must, however, be able to evaluate and monitor the moral decisions of their groups and their leaders, because even as followers, we have a moral duty not to be involved in an immoral enterprise.

---

1. Georgetown University Press (Washington, D.C., 1999), p.75.
2. Cf. "'Tis better to have loved and lost than never to have loved at all." "In Memoriam A.H.H."

The first step to be taken in any valid attempt to oppose evil is that of identifying it. We need to be as certain as possible that what we are opposing is immoral; because should this not be the case, then we ourselves might, in fact, be doing something wrong. And it is not always easy to be sure of this, especially in a world that presents us with fast-changing and continually shifting situations which demand ethical responses. If we are not at least relatively certain that what we are opposing is indeed immoral, then it may be our duty to keep an open mind and to remain tolerant of differing assessments of the situation. In this context, we do not have an ethical duty to oppose what others may be doing unless they are clearly causing or going to cause some unjust harm.

The analysis of what appears to be an evil action should begin by gathering available information. We need to ask who the parties are—particularly the potential perpetrator(s) and the potential victim(s). What are they doing in this regard, or what are they likely to be doing? What are the actual or anticipated consequences of those actions? What group interests may be involved? What are everyone's individual interests and purposes, either as stated and as can be inferred? What, if any, impact might the potential evildoer have on me, on those with whom I share special relationships, or on my primary social groups, both in the short and long term?

Having gathered as much relevant information as possible, we need to bring to bear on it our understanding of evil and other forms of immorality and thereby determine whether the activity in question could fairly be characterized as being morally wrong. In other words, we need to review the information in terms of each of the three essential elements of evil, and then answer the following questions: Would the action be harmful? Would the perpetrator be responsible for it if he carried it out? And would the harm be unjust? It is only when we have answered all three questions in the affirmative that we will have accurately identified an action as immoral.

Whenever we undertake such an analysis, we will probably conclude that the potential action would be harmful. Potential harm is what normally triggers a suspicion that an evil is impending. However, things are not always what they first appear to be, so we need to look carefully for indications of real and substantial harm that might result from the action.

It is also likely that, by the time we have become engaged in the analysis of some potential evil, we will find that the harm would indeed be unjust—that the person who is likely to be victimized has done nothing to warrant it, and that nothing in the larger situation would warrant it, either. To be sure that we are not missing something in our analysis, however, we should consider the different types of things that might make a harm just.

Some of the time spent in the analysis of some impending evil would also need to be devoted to its second element, namely, the question of who might possibly be responsible for it. To ascertain this, we have to establish that the person who is performing the act in question, or who might perform it, is indeed the person who would be the actual cause of the unjust harm.

If our analysis reveals that all three of the elements are present (at least to some degree), we can tentatively conclude that the act in question would be immoral. However, because of the entanglements and negative consequences that follow choosing something which should not, in fact, be opposed, we should take additional precautions before embarking on any such effort. The most important of these involves checking the facts and assessments that we have made with others whose ethics we know to be sound. Not only might they be aware of important additional facts that should be considered, but their skill at assessing the ethical content of the situation may also be significant. External authorities are important resources in the process of validating ethical conclusions for a good reason: They are accomplished in this field, as experts generally are, and their judgments are often correct. There are, of course, limitations to this claim. Sometimes our most egregious failures at opposing evil involve collective decisions fueled by fear or suspicion, both of which become worse when they are reinforced by those who are recognized as moral authorities. There are also cases in which a single individual turns out to have been right and the rest of a group wrong, demonstrating that the counsel of others is not always definitive. Being able to judge correctly whether we should proceed alone (or virtually alone) is a special skill as well, for which personal experience may serve as a guide. It also helps significantly if we have developed an effective moral conscience. Our ethical intuitions are a meaningful source of confirmation of matters of moral truth.

Another precaution we should take is that of reviewing our own motivation for becoming involved in such circumstances in the first place. We should try to be sure that we are not simply looking for an excuse to cause someone else harm. This issue is of particular importance when we recognize that we are relying on a given means/ends test, because so much evil is done in the name of good. As Robert White states in *The Moral Animal*,[3] "A good starting point would be to generally discount moral indignation by 50 percent or so, mindful of its built-in bias, and to be similarly suspicious of moral indifference to suffering."

One of the biggest problems we have in identifying an act as one that we may feel obligated to oppose is the fact that events often move so quickly that we have to make decisions before we have all the information necessary for a proper assessment of them. This can make matters particularly difficult when we know that relevant information is available and accessible somewhere else, because then we will want more time to try to get it. The risk inherent in such a situation is that the immoral act might be carried out before we could obtain those additional facts. In other words, as with many things in life, we may have to make these decisions based upon incomplete data; and when we do, the chances of our making a mistake are multiplied. Such dilemmas are evidenced most dramatically in events whose timing is beyond our control (e.g., when a police officer has but an instant in which to decide whether a suspect is pulling out a gun or a cell phone). Sometimes, however, we simply may not be able to wait for more assurance about our assessments of evil, and we will have to infer it as best we can from what we do know. If, like Hamlet, we sit and wait, and then try to justify our indecision on grounds of incomplete information, the opportunity to prevent the occurrence or continuation of some evil action may disappear altogether.

In situations in which evil has not yet occurred or has not yet completely occurred, it is sometimes helpful to focus on the impending harm which the victim will likely suffer and on whether the harm would be unjust. If those two elements exist, then we may

---

3. Pantheon (New York, 1994), p. 343.

have a duty to act benevolently to help prevent an adverse outcome—*regardless of whether or not the perpetrator is or would be responsible for it.* In other words, if we confirm that the harm and the lack of justness elements are present, then it may not matter whether the third element is. If we are in a position to prevent an impending unjust harm, then we should do so, regardless of its cause. If the harm has not yet begun or been completed, and if we *can* have an impact on the situation, then we should try to prevent the adverse outcome.

The issue of moral responsibility for a given action becomes more important, however, when we are concerned with actions which have already been completed or with actions that may occur in the future but are not yet imminent. With the former, time is usually not a factor in deciding, for example, whether justice requires a punishment. In the latter case, we would have some time left during which we can attempt to discern in advance the presence or absence of moral responsibility. Ongoing and imminent actions, however, present us with more difficulty when responsibility is not obvious. Either we will have to try to make a culpability assessment quickly, or we will have to try to prevent harm from being done to an undeserving person regardless of who may be causing it and regardless of whether anyone may be culpable for it. But before we act in such situations, we should at least try to be sure that the impending harm is unjust, in order to avoid the unpleasant consequences that would flow from making *that* mistake.

We face another problem in "choosing our battles" against evil because of its prevalence. Because immorality is so common, we cannot possibly address all of it; but, on the other hand, we cannot become so discouraged by the immensity of the task that we concede defeat by doing nothing at all. Rather, we need to decide which problems we may be able to help address ourselves, given our limited time, capacities and resources. For just as we have a duty to act benevolently by doing charity at least some of the time, so we also have a benevolence duty to try to prevent the infliction of unjust harm at least some of the time.

Our decisions in this area necessarily involve several different considerations. The first is exigency. If some evil action is threatened and imminent or is being carried out right in front of our eyes, and particularly if we are the only one present who might be able to stop it, then the circumstances themselves will essentially have imposed upon us a moral responsibility for doing so. If, however, immediate action is not required, we will have some time in which to prioritize the ethical issues which are most important to us, based upon what seems to be most needed and upon where our personal efforts might be most effective.

How we can try to deal with evil and other forms of immorality can vary somewhat depending upon the point to which it has progressed—whether it is impending, ongoing or completed. Regardless of which of these may be the case, our efforts are generally more effective if they are well planned. Such planning should include an inventory of the resources necessary for a successful outcome and the development of strategic alternatives.

A variety of strategic options can be employed in these efforts. For all but completed evils, direct dissuasions, which may consist of arguments alone or may include promised rewards for not doing evil or threatened punishments if the evil is done or even attempted, may be effective. Threatened punishments may include such things as exposure or threatened exposure (if that might cause harm or give pause to the perpetrator) or a variety of other justified harms. A second alternative is the removal or protection of the "prize" so that doing the evil will not bring the perpetrator his desired "reward." The third principal option is direct confrontation—using whatever forceful means might be effective in stopping the evildoer from carrying out his or her wrongful actions.

All intentional behavior can be affected by anticipated rewards and punishments. Exactly what form those may need to take in order to effectively dissuade someone from engaging in an immoral act depends primarily on both the character and nature of the perpetrator and on the resources available to be used as rewards and punishments. There is little to restrain our imaginations in formulating effective alternative deterrents, but what should restrain our consideration of these alternatives are the ethics of the options. Would the proposed enticement or detriment be excessive or morally wrong in some way?[4] If so, we need to move on to other potentially effective alternatives. The range of options available to us may also enhance the possibility of resolving or ameliorating some of these problems through negotiation, arbitration or mediation.

People who do wrong are almost always trying to gain something or to benefit in some way. As we try to understand the larger social dynamics of such actions, it helps to remember that *someone* almost always benefits from every bad thing that happens in our world.[5] When confronting a situation which involves some sort of immoral activity, we need to ask who would benefit, and in what way. If those receiving the benefits are the ones doing the harm, then eliminating the "reward," or making it inaccessible, might effectively interdict the wrongful behavior.

A third strategic option in efforts to stop wrongdoing is directly confronting an evildoer with some sort of force that would be sufficient to prevent his success. This can be accomplished in different ways as well. Physical resistance or violent force can be used, as, for example, through a policeman's nightstick. Displays of power can often produce the same result (e.g., by filling the streets with foot patrolmen to diminish neighborhood crime). This type of force is physical, and many weapons and defensive systems are used when we have violent engagements. A considerable number of guidelines have been developed on how to effectively plan or strategize, which can be used not only in military but also in nonmilitary settings.[6]

But other kinds of force can be employed in confronting evil actions as well, including what is referred to as "moral force." Effective deterrence may be provided through the types of nonviolence advanced by Mahatma Gandhi or by Martin Luther King.

---

4. Chamberlain's sacrifice of Czechoslovakia to Hitler serves as one of the most vivid historical examples of an inappropriate appeasement that was also ineffective.
5. Contractors and suppliers benefit from hurricanes and tornados; hospitals and medical personnel (and sometimes lawyers) benefit from injuries; and so on.
6. For example, *The Art of Warfare* by Sun-Tzu, *Principles of War* by Carl von Clausewitz, and *Strategy* by B. H. Liddell Hart.

Strength may also be exercised through directly employed goodness (e.g., Romans 12:21: "Do not let evil defeat you; instead, conquer evil with good"). Our strategic options for direct engagements with people who are doing something evil, or threatening to do so, may therefore encompass a fairly wide range of nonviolent alternatives.[7]

In every such situation it is imperative that we make a preliminary assessment of the strength of the evildoer(s). This means reviewing all the forms of power that may be available for their use, including actual and potential support from others. Alternative actions that might diminish or prevent some or all of that potential or actual support should regularly be taken into consideration. This could involve something as minimal as exposing the evil nature of a plan, or it might require something as significant as mobilizing a major direct threat of force poised to act against the evildoer's supporters. Since most intentional evils are "buttressed" by erroneous means/ends arguments, if the defects in those arguments can be effectively communicated to the supporters, it could undermine their confidence in the rectitude of their cause. Intensive efforts to confront the supporters of evildoers are necessary because any diminution in that support can substantially impact the outcome of the situation; for if the supporters of evildoers fade away, sometimes their plans do, too.

Once we have decided on our general strategies for dealing with something which we feel compelled to oppose, we need to engage in even more detailed planning and preparation. After reviewing the various strategic alternatives, we should put together a practical plan which is sound enough to succeed if all things go as expected. It should also be flexible enough to allow us to employ alternatives if and when things begin to go poorly. Part of this process involves determining the degree of effort which should be given to the opposition or prevention of a particular evil. We may have to decide whether we should use our greatest force against this potential evil or whether we should employ some lesser force and save the former for potentially greater evils which might occur some other day

---

7. See, for example, the list of 198 methods of nonviolent action in *The Politics of Nonviolent Action*, Gene Sharp, Porter Sargeant Publishers (Boston, 1973).

(particularly if that maximum force is in any way nonrenewable). It is, on the other hand, most regrettable when an effort to prevent some act of evil fails because of an inaccurate assessment of the amount of force necessary to do so, particularly if additional force was, in fact, available and could have altered the outcome. We also need to know who our allies are and how much they might be able and willing to assist us. Because evil can be synergistic (the amount of wrong that members of a determined group can do can be greater than the sum of their individual abilities to do wrong), those who would confront evil often need to bring their own combined strength to bear in order to meet and defeat the collective strength of wrongdoers. Therefore, we have to ascertain what it might take to get our potential allies to become involved. This means determining their levels of interest in the issues at hand and knowing what might motivate them to participate in the effort.

If we have had the opportunity to formulate a plan and have done so, we are then in a position to implement it. Its details have to be communicated to and understood by its supporters. Then the plan must be executed, either defensively (in response to an action of the evildoer), or offensively (when it becomes clear that the potential evildoer has not been and will not be deterred except by preemptive action). Once it has been set in motion, the plan needs to be carried out, with the necessary adjustments to meet unanticipated contingencies. It is advisable regularly to consider ways to increase the number of people who actively support the effort by trying to encourage others to become involved in it. At some point, however, many of these endeavors are reduced to matters of resolve and perseverance. As in sporting events, those who prevail are often the groups that have the greater desire to win and the greater willingness to work harder and longer in order to reach their goals. Therefore, we need to try to increase, or at least maintain, not only our own dedication, but also the motivation and perseverance of our compatriots.

After having implemented a plan, we have to recognize when it is appropriate to end our effort. Throughout both the planning and the implementation processes, we should have been considering the alternative outcomes. In addition to victories or defeats, there can also be draws. Compromises avoid defeats. They save resources for another day and another effort. They sometimes can lead to better long-term resolutions, because total defeats often do not end disputes entirely or permanently. Vengefulness frequently ensues following a defeat, as can a justifiable resistance to new oppression. Extended common efforts to implement an acceptable compromise may therefore be the most effective way of terminating some of these confrontations.

When we are winning, decisions about what to do next will usually be the easiest. When we are not winning, these decisions may be more difficult. Yet we need to understand that we will not win all of our battles against evil—particularly in cases in which it has a great force. Taking a longer-term view of the situation may sometimes require us to compromise or even concede. Few examples of great success in such confrontations were not preceded by numerous defeats along the way. If we are vanquished, we will subsequently not be able to do anything at all; so we may sometimes have to take the risk of suffering at least temporary losses along the way.

Finally, after our efforts have been concluded, and regardless of the outcome, we usually have some post-confrontation responsibilities, as well. Ethical reconstruction is an obligation that we incur if we have destroyed or damaged something in the process, whether we have won or lost the battle. What we do "the morning after" can sometimes have as much impact on the future as whatever we may have accomplished in successfully opposing a given evil. Post-confrontation issues always involve our responsibility to act benevolently—to do justice and be charitable. But they also include consideration of how to effectively sustain opposition to and suppression of the type of evil which we have been confronting (if we have been successful). If we have not succeeded, decisions will need to be made about whether we should modify our objectives or tactics.

In handling our post-confrontation responsibilities, we should proceed along the same general lines as we did in our initial opposition to evil. We need to: (a) assess the situation, including the circumstances and needs of those who were involved; (b) consider the various options for ethical reconstruction, together with their advantages and disadvantages; (c) review the practicalities, particularly the resources and the people who would have to be involved; (d) choose a plan; and (e) implement it.

Strategies for dealing with situations in which no specific harm is imminent but general conditions exist that somehow increase the likelihood of the occurrence of some type of harm have to be handled somewhat differently. One approach to preventing specific manifestations of harm when such a general threat exists—particularly when the harm might not be intentionally caused—is to make potential harmdoers more aware of the possibility that certain kinds of behavior may tend to lead to unjust harm (e.g., "The roads are icy, slow down if you're driving!"). If people are motivated to avoid causing unjust harm (i.e., if they have any degree of benevolence whatsoever), they will be more likely to be cautious and less likely to cause such harm carelessly if they are informed about the increased potential for harm that exists in these situations. Safety campaigns, for example, which can be directed toward groups or specific individuals, combine education and training with exhortations to vigilance. Another aspect of such preventative efforts would be to remind potential harmdoers of the negative consequences that would follow careless acts that caused such harm, for the deterrence that might provide.

Our efforts at prevention can also include attempts to encourage general character improvement on group levels. This would involve fostering good character and general respect for morality, on the one hand, and reducing bad character and diminishing general indifference toward or disrespect for morality, on the other hand. Preventing bad character problems usually begins with those upon whom we have the most direct influence—with our children (in the case of parents), or siblings and other close relatives, or friends. Like most other things, character development can, to some extent, be facilitated by appropriate rewards and/or punishments on both personal and group levels.

Generally speaking, good character development on a large scale appears to require certain conditions, or at least it seems likely to be maximized only when certain conditions are met. Direct correlations appear to exist between the proper cultivation of good character and several general group characteristics, including social stability, a respect for and a tolerance of religion within the group (including, if more than one religion is practiced within a group, a tolerance for the diverse religions), and a general shared acceptance of basic moral beliefs. An inverse correlation may be discerned with regard to some other types of group, including those that suffer from oppressive or ineffectual governments or those experiencing substantial instability within their major social systems, or those in which there is either a widespread disrespect for religious diversity or a general disbelief in or rejection of basic moral principles. Reasonable efforts to improve our larger groups in any of these areas would probably move individual group members toward better characters and away from poorer characters, as well.

The general moral climate within any group can be measured in a variety of ways. A cursory measure of it would look at a few readily available pieces of information—crime statistics, for example, or the individual character of the group's formal and informal leaders. Surveys can more comprehensively reflect the members' perceptions about a number of ethical indicators that can help with an assessment of the general or prevailing level of the group's morality and the frequency of moral breaches within the group. A comprehensive analysis of this sort could include various measurements aimed at establishing the group's general location along the moral continuums discussed above, such as determining collective degrees of restraint exercised in the pursuit of pleasure and in the avoidance of pain, of self-actualization, of the performance of duty of fidelity, or the fulfilling of our regular obligation to act benevolently.

It can be argued that, to some extent, general levels of ethics wax and wane. The degree of general morality that is exercised within a group certainly appears to fluctuate over time. Sometimes it seems that people are acting in a manner that is more moral, but at other times, it appears that they are behaving less morally. Whether these fluctuations involve any regularity and the extent to which they can be influenced and might be responsive to concerted intentional efforts is a matter of debate. At the very least, however, unless a large number of people keep trying to avoid doing wrong things, those periods in which positive moral development is a prevalent feature of social life will neither be as strong nor as persistent as they could otherwise have been. Moreover, those in which negative moral developments occur with respect to public morality will be longer and more difficult than they otherwise would need to be.

We must therefore confront evil and other forms of immorality not only on individual and small group levels, but also with an eye toward impacting more of the world as a whole—i.e., taking a sort of "macromoral" view of it. This can lead to efforts within our major groups that are aimed at the systemic development of good character and the suppression of bad character. Individually, we can most easily become involved in these endeavors by supporting or affiliating ourselves with those groups which seek to establish and maintain economic and political justice, stability, and respect for religions and basic moral values.

Our options for opposing evil actions that have already been carried out are obviously more limited—particularly when we have only become involved at that point. Since prevention will no longer be an option because some unjust harm will already have been done, opposing evil in this context means seeking justice for all concerned. With regard to the perpetrator, this may involve imposing some punishment or exacting some sort of reparations. With regard to the victim, justice may involve providing aid and comfort combined with imposing some sort of retributive harm on the perpetrator(s).

The question of what constitutes appropriate punishment and/or reparations is complex. What might be effective and yet not excessive punishment depends in great part on the social context and history of a particular group. There are times, however, when we must impose punishments on or exact reparations from wrongdoers, or we will find that we have failed to prevent future evils of the same kind. In other words, carrots do not always work; sometimes only sticks do. If we do not deter someone from performing an evil action when we are in a position to do so, we may be violating important ethical duties that we have to those who may, in the future, be victims of similar unjust harms.

Furthermore, every major social group has a responsibility to determine whether it might be able to do something other than, or in addition to, punishment as part of an effort to prevent wrongdoing, for the threat of punishment is not always an effective deterrent. Such an effort requires an understanding of all of the direct and indirect reasons why such unjust harm or harms have occurred. To a considerable extent, every society is responsible for the ethical development and moral rectitude of its members. When it can positively affect those things, and when it can eliminate or reduce the conditions that tend to lead some of its members to engage in wrongdoing, its leaders have an obligation to promote and institute such changes.

Punishments imposed by our governments can take various forms. Formal criminal punishments usually consist of the deprivation of freedom or property. Freedoms can be restricted in many ways, from incarceration to certain limitations on activities or associations. Deprivation of property usually takes the form of fines, but it can also include other sorts of exactions (e.g., the seizure of cars or boats used in drug-smuggling operations). Governments sometimes go beyond restricting freedom or exacting fines or confiscating property, however, for they also have the power to impose corporeal types of criminal punishment (such as whippings or executions). Governments can additionally utilize non-criminal sanctions against wrongdoers. If, for example, a license or other type of official permit is necessary in order to do something, such as practicing a profession or constructing a building, the government can punish us by withholding or revoking it.

Private punishments are allowed through governmental forums in most parts of the world through civil reparations systems. Individuals and groups who have been unjustly harmed may make use of courts or other tribunals to seek monetary damages from the wrongdoers as compensation for their injuries.

Forms of punishment which are not governmentally administered can also be imposed by other types of social groups. Every such group has the ability to discipline its members in one way or another, formally or informally. Suspension and expulsion are viable options for many of them. While a few groups may not be able to utilize these sanctions completely (e.g., a family), they can still do so functionally (e.g., by cutting off contacts with an offending sibling). If a social organization has strong ties with its members, the disciplinary sanctions which it may impose can be every bit as severe as governmentally levied punishments (e.g., excommunication from a church).

Finally, a single individual or a small group may sometimes appropriately punish another person or persons. Such penalties may be particularly warranted when the original harm is relatively insignificant (i.e., too minor to be either detected or addressed by government or other social organizations). Disciplinary measures imposed by some individuals on others can include any of the types of harm that were discussed previously with regard to innocent victims. In these cases, however, a suitable level of harm would be deserved punishment, and therefore would not be unjust.

When others are doing things that are evil or otherwise immoral, we can be passive observers or we can be active participants in efforts to confront them and try to make things right. The latter option is the only way to fulfill our general ethical duty to try to make the world a better place.

Opposing evils that others might do, are doing or have done, is rarely an easy task. It requires that we become involved in conflicts, and it causes us to risk suffering, deprivation and defeat. Yet we must persist in this, at least at times. If we shrink from this responsibility, we not only risk greater suffering, deprivation and defeat over the long term, but also the moral diminishment of ourselves and of our world.

The Ethical Choices for Victims

The first sections of this chapter have addressed the confrontation of evil by resisting and attempting to defeat it. Such actions can be taken by almost anyone, regardless of their roles or positions—whether they are victims, possible victims, potential perpetrators, friends, co-conspirators, or bystanders. In addition, however, victims have several other choices which merit special consideration.

The range of options presented to us as victims or possible victims varies with the timing of the harmful act. We have one set of choices for our responses to threatened evil, another for responses to evil that is presently occurring, and a third for responding after the unjust harm has already been done. For threatened evil that may be impending, our choices include taking some direct action to try to prevent it from happening (e.g., by launching a preemptive strike or otherwise disrupting the plans of the agent), improving our defenses to protect ourselves in case an actual attack is carried out later, or doing nothing at all. At the moment harm is actually being done we can either put up resistance and fight, or not. Once the unjust harm has already been done, our options vary with the outcome. For people who have successfully resisted or avoided the evil (or most of it) and who have suffered no more than minimal harm (because most or all of the threatened harm never occurred), the choices are whether to do something further about the problem or not. This usually means determining whether to seek punishment or some other sanction against the unsuccessful wrongdoers, or not. Those who have actually been harmed in some significant way, however, face a different set of choices, including not only whether to seek punishment through our systems of social controls, but also whether to pursue reparations or to try to exact personal revenge, or whether to do none of these.

When assessing the "ethicalness" of our potential responses to evildoers from the position of the victim, we need to focus primarily on our obligations of benevolence and loyalty, since these essentially govern how we are to treat other people. An evaluation from the benevolence perspective requires that we determine first what the other person's "due" is—what would constitute a just solution to the problem for him or her, under the circumstances. One of our benevolence duties is to do justice, and another is not to do injustice. The beginning point for such an assessment is understanding what would be just and unjust with regard to the incident at hand. In doing so, we must necessarily rely upon comparable events within our respective social groups. What have others done, or had done to them, in roughly parallel cases? Precedents can serve as guides in our search for consensus on general standards to be used when imposing penalties for injustices. We can also test our own judgment of the situation for impartiality by asking ourselves whether we would find the same disciplinary measure appropriate if we had been the wrongdoers. If our answer is in the negative, then the proposed resolution might need some adjustment.

However, the analysis should not end at this point. We also need to consider the situation in light of the issue of fidelity, because of our responsibilities to those with whom we share special relationships. Parents of both the victim and the perpetrator are, for instance, morally obligated to stand behind their children and support them (at least to some extent), with very few exceptions. Furthermore, we may have a unique obligation of loyalty to one of the groups involved in the incident by virtue of our membership in it (i.e., either the group of the victim or that of the wrongdoer). We all bear responsibility, at least to some degree, for our group's collective safety and well-being; and, for this reason, we may need to revise our assessment in order, for example, to help deter others from similar offenses and thereby protect other members of our group from similar adverse consequences.

After this analysis has been completed, we will likely find that we have at our disposal a range of potential responses that would all do justice in the situation, at least to some degree. Determining the specific type and intensity of the punishment or other sanctions to impose may, however, involve further considerations, even though any outcome within the range that we have defined as appropriate would be considered just and thus essentially the wrongdoer's "due."

Deciding what justice would require of us in these situations may not end our consideration of these matters because another aspect of benevolence, as we have previously noted, is charity. Mercy is a form of charity. In order to be ethically balanced, we should be charitable, at least some of the time; and, hence, at least sometimes, we should also be merciful.

We show mercy to another person when we choose not to impose what has been determined to be a legitimate and appropriate sanction, or when we choose not to impose the full extent of the harm of a sanction which would then otherwise be due. We usually associate merciful actions or choices with those who have an ethical option to cause justified harm to another, which includes victims, who may or may not seek revenge or reparations, and certain of our authorities, who may or may not choose to assess punishments on behalf of our groups.

Mercy is thus the foregoing or the intentional omission of a harmful action which we would be justified in taking. While we can be said to "act" when we show mercy, it is more precisely described as something that we do not do. We are merciful when we do not impose a punishment on someone, or when we do not impose the severest kind of punishment that justice would allow, in circumstances in which we could legitimately do either of these things (and perhaps normally ought to do, if that is what justice would then require). When we do—or do not do—something along these lines for reasons of benevolence, we are being merciful. (We can forebear for other, non-benevolent reasons, of course, such as for personal gain from a bribe; but that kind of forbearance is not mercy.[8])

Both external and internal considerations contribute to the assessment of the propriety of merciful behavior in particular situations. External factors include: demonstrated remorse on the part of the wrongdoer and some indication as to whether he has "learned his lesson"; any actions voluntarily undertaken by the wrongdoer to repair or ameliorate the harm; the general character of the wrongdoer (which may be discerned in part by determining whether the action under review was an isolated event); whether any special social reasons exist that would require us to be merciful; the victim's attitude toward a merciful solution, as well as the attitudes of his or her primary social groups; whether acting mercifully here and now might help or hurt those who might be victims in the future; and, finally, what impact a merciful solution to the situation might have on larger social groups and on the levels of their own cohesion.

Internal factors affecting such a decision can also have an impact on whether we will seek either a lesser punishment (or no punishment at all) or fewer reparations (or none) from someone who has done us some unjust harm. To begin with, as a victim or a potential victim, we will feel anger and fear and oftentimes some confusion, as well (as demonstrated by the "Why me?" question which we tend

---

8. Similarly, we do not associate mercy with forbearance on the part of evildoers, such as someone who decides at the last minute not to beat up someone he is also robbing; because while they may have the power to impose further harm, they do not have the right to do so. That kind of "forbearance" is much lower in the benevolence scale; its limited ethical credit comes from not doing yet another and perhaps greater injustice and from not causing yet another harm.

to ask of all harm that is headed our way, whether it is the work of some wrongdoer or not). In addition, when actual harm has been done to us, we suffer both physically and mentally. And, even after the actual harmful act has ended, we have to deal with the emotional consequences of it—with the other and often deeper wounds inflicted on us by doers of evil: hostility, withdrawal, vengefulness, hatred and other residual emotional damage which may linger in our psyche as a result of the attack. But the most significant internal factor affecting a decision about whether to be merciful is forgiveness.

Forgiveness is primarily an emotional decision that we can make in response to the person or persons who have harmed us. Forgiveness is the cessation and relinquishment of anger and resentment, and it creates a mental state or attitude that makes merciful actions possible. It is the emotional impetus for our exacting less than we could legitimately be expected to demand from someone who has unjustly harmed us.

While forgiveness may be encouraged, and while attempts may be made to induce it, real forgiveness cannot be forced, because it is an internal event which requires our conscious recognition and assent. Anger and resentment cannot always be quelled upon demand. Furthermore, while a less than fully embraced act of forgiveness may lead to a merciful action, it would not then be followed by internal reconciliation and emotional healing.

Forgiving is an option not only for those directly victimized by the evil or otherwise immoral acts, but also for those who have been secondarily harmed because of their close relationships with the victims (e.g., the family and friends of a person who has been assaulted). Whenever an individual is unjustly harmed, his or her group is also adversely affected, to some extent. And anyone who has been harmed is in a position to forgive the agent who caused that harm.

Forgiveness is, nevertheless, essentially a personal matter. We can forgive someone for the harm that he or she has caused us, but we cannot fully forgive someone for the harm that he or she may have caused to others. Moreover, we can show mercy toward wrongdoers only to the extent that we have some power and possess some right to exact punishment or reparations. In the absence of these, we may still recommend forgiveness and mercy to others, however, and thus facilitate the process of their forgiveness. Such recommendations may be significant, for people become more forgiving by associating with others who are generous in this manner, and by reflecting on the times that they have been forgiven by others and what those responses have meant to them.

Forgiveness has both negative and positive aspects. Negatively characterized, it is a decision not to hate or not to hold on to animosity toward a wrongdoer. This is often followed by the abandonment of any desire to cause justified harm to the perpetrator or to pursue the imposition of punishment on or to seek reparations from the wrongdoer. In positive terms, it is a decision to move on with our lives and to release ourselves from the negative aftereffects of the evil done to us, and from the internal suffering that almost invariably ensues.

We can forgive others privately—in our hearts—and not let anyone else know about it. Usually, however, an act of forgiveness is one that is communicated to others. Even when we do not verbally inform anyone about it ourselves, the fact that we have forgiven someone for injuring us unjustly tends to make itself evident in other ways (for example, through the fact that the victim is not trying to have the perpetrator punished). It is, however, when forgiveness is communicated directly to the evildoer that it has its greatest impact on all concerned.

There are a number of types of reasons why we should generally be forgiving, and why mercy should naturally follow upon forgiveness. Even if we are not usually inclined to be merciful, however, we should at least sometimes be so; because in order to be ethically balanced (which, I submit, is the key to essential morality), we need to be charitable at least some of the time. Other philosophical reasons to forgive are because it represents a positive ethical response, as opposed to the negative ethical response, to harm and suffering. Having a forgiving nature and being forgiven are aspects of the positive ground of being, whereas being unforgiving in nature and being unforgiven are aspects of the negative ground. Furthermore, forgiveness at appropriate times and in appropriate circumstances helps us fulfill our obligations of both loyalty and benevolence to others. It can lead to major transformations for the better in an evildoer. Many misdirected lives have been turned around as a result of forgiveness given and mercy shown. Finally, forgiveness can be justified philosophically by the fact that its regular employment leads to a more ethical world, while its moral opposite—vengefulness— simply leads to more violence and evil.

There are strong psychological reasons to be forgiving, as well. Our negative reactions to some unjust harm that has been inflicted upon us by the immoral actions of others can consume us mentally and often, ultimately, physically as well. Anger, rage, hatred and longing for revenge all poison us from within and crowd out the opportunities we may have to achieve and maintain a healthy and balanced psychic state. It is only when we have freed ourselves from the adverse psychological consequences of the evil that has been done to us that we can really get on with the rest of our lives.[9] The refusal to forgive, or the failure to do so, can lead to imbalance, stress, withdrawal, and bodily harm.

Substantial conformity exists among the world's religions on the question of the need for forgiveness. Jesus taught the importance of our being willing to forgive by word (e.g., Forgive "not seven times, but seventy times seven"—Matthew 18:22) and by deed (e.g., by forgiving his killers from the cross—Luke 23:34). The willingness to forgive others has thus become one of the central values of the Christian faith. Buddhists are instructed to follow the virtuous paths of kindness to others and the avoidance of hatred, as reflected in the story of a Buddhist prince who spared the life of the murderer of his family because of his father's dying admonition that "hatred is not appeased by hatred; hatred is appeased by non-hatred alone."[10] Practitioners of Islam are also directed to be compassionate and hence forgiving in appropriate situations. It is written in the Koran: "And the recompense of evil is punishment like it, but whoever forgives and amends, he shall have his reward from Allah; surely He

---

9.   See, e.g., *Forgiving the Unforgivable*, Beverly Flanigan, Macmillan Publishing Co. (New York, 1992).
10.   Quoted from *Mahavagga* X.ii.3-20 in "'As We Forgive': Interhuman Forgiveness in The Teaching of Jesus," George Soares-Prabhu, *Forgiveness*, Casiano Floristan and Christian Duquoc, ed., T. & T. Clark Ltd. (Edinburgh, 1986), p. 57.

does not love the unjust."[11] In the Bhagavad Gita, the following observation guides Hindus: "Splendor, forgiveness, fortitude, cleanliness, absence of malice, and absence of pride; these are qualities of those endowed with divine virtues, O Arjuna."[12] In short, there are substantial religious as well as philosophical and psychological reasons for forgiving others for the unjust harms that they cause us.

As a practical matter, we cannot live well among others without practicing at least some degree of forgiveness, given the frequency with which harmful incidents seem to occur. Forgiveness facilitates cooperation, while the pervasive absence of a spirit of forgiveness can create friction and thus interfere with social interaction and development.

While we thus have a number of reasons for forgiving those who injure us, there are also some reasons *not* to forgive in certain situations—or at least, not to forgive when the issue first arises. We would violate our obligation generally to act benevolently toward others, and specifically our obligation to act benevolently toward the victims of unjust harm, if we were to forgive the perpetrator while he or she was in the act of doing something evil to the victim, for that could abet the continuation of that evil act. We would also be wrong to forgive wrongdoers if doing so would facilitate their engaging in additional evil acts (e.g., those for whom an expectation of forgiveness would either nullify or diminish the deterrent power of the threat of punishment). In addition, while positive changes in an evildoer can be reinforced by acts of forgiveness, and thus future harmful actions might be averted by a present mercifulness, if the wrongdoer shows neither remorse nor any desire to change, it becomes more difficult (and less rational) to forgive. Consequently, immediately forgiving every wrong that may be done to us would be ethically inappropriate.

Even when we believe that we have a good reason to decline to forgive someone, it might nevertheless be proper to reconsider that decision at some later point in time. If we delay in making a final decision until some things which were potential problems have been

---

11. 42.40.
12. Chapter 16, Verse 3.

addressed or have disappeared, we can revisit the issue later and determine whether a change of heart might be warranted. The passage of time can also help us overcome some of the negative emotional responses that might be blocking our current path toward forgiveness. On the other hand, if we want to complete an act of forgiveness by making it known to the person being forgiven, we also cannot wait too long. Sometimes the opportunity to conclude such an act by communicating it to the perpetrator is lost simply by the passage of time (e.g., one party or the other may be deceased by then).

The commonly expressed objection that mercy can allow an offender to escape from justice, and that it would therefore be an injustice to be merciful, may be relevant in some cases. However, we should look at justice not only in the context of the specific case at hand but also from a larger perspective. If we do not take this broader view of it, we run the risk of doing injustice to others by rigidly considering their actions only in isolation. But actions simply do not occur only in isolation. We also need to review a number of factors external to the action being considered, such as whether the imposition of a proposed punishment would cause some sort of harm not only to the offender, but perhaps also to others, or whether it would interfere with the larger group's obligation to provide equal justice. If a person who caused some unjust harm subsequently and voluntarily made effective reparations and prevented a similar harm from occurring to someone else, then our failure to forgive and to grant mercy (at least to some extent) would constitute a violation of our general obligation to act benevolently. In other words, if we look at the larger context of the situation, an offender's "due" *can* be changed. Because of these factors, judicial systems and social institutions must be allowed to exercise a certain amount of discretion in the imposition of punishment; they must be able to consider the situation from a larger perspective and to try to anticipate the impact that the various alternatives would have on all concerned.[13]

---

13. It is in this context that it is appropriate to discuss mercy in our criminal justice systems, and not just leniency and pardon. Judges who act mercifully after considering the larger ethical impact of the various alternative punishments are acting justly, and not unjustly.

Like most other things, forgiveness can be a matter of degree. We can forgive fully, only a little, or somewhere in between. Our willingness to forgive can change over time. If an action is substantially evil, forgiveness may be impossible for all but the most charitable among us. Complete forgiveness may also be inappropriate if it emanates either from a lack of self-respect or from a deficient sense of self-worth on the part of the forgiver, since neither of these would evidence a healthy or ethically balanced individual psyche. When everything is forgiven, nothing is demanded; and when nothing is demanded, the consequences are valuelessness and anarchy.

A decision to grant mercy should not always have to be justified by an offender's repentance or reparations. Justifications or other reasons provided in support of forgiving someone may make it more appropriate and more likely for mercy to occur; but if mercy is an act of charity, then it need not be justified by anything more than the desire of the forgiver to act benevolently. We do not require a justification (other than obvious economic need) from a beggar before giving him alms; similarly, we should not require any justification (beyond an obvious need for forgiveness) before we are willing to practice this aspect of charity which we call "mercy." Consequently, it is incorrect to condemn forgiveness and mercy on the basis of the argument that they undermine justice in cases in which no separate, external justification for them exists. Besides, even in the bleakest of human situations, mercy can bring about repentance at some later point, and hence can also lead to acts of goodness from the (former) evildoer, or from other individuals.

In sum, the ethics of victimhood involves much more than self-defense and consideration of the different degrees of force which may justifiably be brought to bear in the confrontation of evil. It also requires acknowledgment and consideration of justice, forgiveness and mercy, and, in appropriate cases, it constrains us to forgive those who have transgressed against us, and show them mercy.

Conclusions and Caveats

If you are inclined to challenge evil somehow, you can do so in many different ways. Hopefully, however, you will confront it with due consideration. When many of us confront evil, we often do so emotionally and almost reflexively, so that reason seems to play only a small part in our response to it. While I have spent the second portion of this book exhorting the reader to actively resist and defeat evil, I here find myself compelled to add, "But be careful!" So many moral confrontations that were intended to make the world a better place—or at least a less evil place—seem to have gone awry.

We need to understand the facts, we need context, we need perspective . . . in other words, we need to work at getting our moral endeavors right. As with all of our other major activities, we can do them well, we can do them poorly, or we can do them somewhere in between. Trying to stay on the right side in these conflicts takes a great deal of effort. It is easier to be lazy, to depend too much on the insights and opinions of others, and to slide along complacently—even though embarking on one of these endeavors might bring us considerable personal difficulties (as well as satisfactions and rewards).

To make sound decisions in this arena of life, we need to understand what makes something immoral, as well as how to resist and attack it. It is also helpful if we can recognize our limitations and, where necessary, reign in some of our initial enthusiasm. We simply make fewer mistakes when we act after we have cooled down and applied some reason, and not just emotion, to the situation.

Furthermore, we need to remember that committing immoral acts (including evil acts) is not only human, but also commonplace. Immorality is always a real choice for every one of us. Strong temptations are constantly present, ever ready to lead us into making wrong moral decisions. Those who do wrong are human beings, too, and often well meaning ones, at that. The fact that someone is in moral error does not mean that he or she is no longer a human being, nor does it mean that the wrongdoer is no longer entitled to basic justice and respectful treatment from others.

It is still and always fine to hate evil; but if we find ourselves hating the evildoer, we place ourselves in moral peril in a number of different ways. First, we have probably lost our perspective on the matter, because few if any people who are hated are *completely* vile. To the contrary, there are things that each of us could appreciate and respect in almost every other person on this planet. Hating the wrongdoer is therefore probably an emotional overreaction, which can, by itself, lead us to commit our own moral errors. It is easier for us to harm other people when they have been dehumanized or even demonized; but if we overreact to them and thereby cause unjustified harm in reaction to their evil, then *we* will also have done a wrong. Secondly, as many of us have learned the hard way, hatred consumes the hater even if the hater is successful in punishing the hated. It is personally destructive to succumb to intense hatred, whether it is well or ill-founded. When hatred is a response to an earlier unjust harm, the initial victim can become corrupted by the force of such hatred alone—thereby providing both the initial harmdoer and evil itself with a sort of double "victory": not only the first wrong perpetrated against the victim, but also an enduring internal process of moral and psychological destruction of the victim. Thirdly, hating the evildoer may prevent some good from occurring, and moral blame can attach to this, as well. It is for this reason that we are told to hate the sin but not the sinner.[14] Reconciliation and redemption are much more likely to occur if we focus on the evil rather than on the evildoer. Redemptions happen; but if we hate the sinners, redemptions will happen less often, and the fault will not always and only lie with the sinners, but also sometimes with those who hate them—those who make redemption so difficult, or who prevent it from occurring at all. Finally, if we hate and exclude from our company those who do wrong, where do we stop? And who would be left to be included in the circle of our love? Internal self-destruction resulting from hatred is best avoided by forgiveness, which is nourished by the understanding that it is possible for even the vilest evildoer to be redeemed, and that even victims of the most terrible evils can rise above the damage and personal degradation that they have suffered through their forgiveness of those who have sinned against them.

The fact that we might be wrong about what we are opposing should also compel us to exercise restraint in our reaction to evil. Misidentifications of evil occur frequently, particularly if we try to

---

14. And indeed, to love the sinner. (Luke 6:27-36)

make them while we are angry or otherwise emotionally upset. If we commit ourselves to a certain moral position too early, it can later be difficult to back away from a set course of action, even when we subsequently realize that it would be better to do so.

We need to regularly remind ourselves that our misjudgments about evil can have numerous problematic consequences. Any damage or destruction that we do in the name of good is harmful, regardless of its impetus; and acts of mistaken ethical destruction are unethical acts. If our supposedly sound reasoning is erroneous, then we have made a moral mistake for which we might not be able to make effective amends. If, for example, we accept a fallacious means/ends argument and there really is no "higher good" in front of us, then when we hurt someone in its counterfeit name, *we* will have done something wrong, regardless of our true intentions.

When measuring our options in the course of any effort to act against evil, we need to remember that we cause additional moral problems when we go to extremes. Even if we are initially right in identifying the evil that we are opposing, we are constrained by ethical limits on our reactions and responses to it. Overreactions simply continue to weave a fabric of evil which we may have had the opportunity to rend. At some point, we must be willing to cease and desist from our efforts to exact revenge in the name of just punishment. It is imperative for us to try to contribute something toward ending the many apparently ceaseless struggles in this world that repetitively perpetuate subsequent evils for prior ones. Unfortunately, overreactions to evil have often caused more moral damage than the initial wrongs that got them started. Great inequities have been done in the name of ostensible good, in part because opposing evil is taken by so many people as providing them with a license to cause harm. Such errors and miscalculations have undoubtedly enlarged the domain of evil, and they allow it to flourish in many situations in which it should otherwise have withered and died.

Having said these things, I offer the following caveats: be careful both in the battles you choose to fight and in the implementations of your strategic plans for them. Make sure, to the best of your ability, that you are not analyzing the situation incorrectly or misidentifying something as evil, so that you can continue to fulfill your own ethical duties. While a major ethical obligation is to confront evil, an even greater one is to avoid doing evil ourselves. A very large part of doing good is simply trying to do no evil. Thus, we need to review from time to time how well we are identifying what is wrong in our world, and we need to encourage others to do this more carefully as well.

Perhaps the quickest and most efficient way to test our moral position in any given situation is by imagining ourselves to be on the other side of it. Empathy really is a great ethical instrument; it is the chisel of justice. We are all wrongdoers at times; some legitimacy may accrue—and often does—to both parties in a moral confrontation. Similarly, there may be ethical illegitimacy in continued opposition and confrontation. Only if we can empathize with the purported wrongdoer and say with assurance that had *we* committed that unjust harm, we would deserve the punishment we now seek to impose on him or her, or that had *we* been threatening to commit a certain unjust harm, we would deserve to have the force we are planning to use be deployed against us, can we argue that we are justified in pursuing the punishments that we now seek to impose or in implementing a certain forceful opposition to a threatened evil. Such a general effort, if it were done honestly, could dramatically diminish the overreactions to evils in our world and thereby reduce the number of incidents of new evil that occur every day—perhaps more than anything else that we could possibly undertake.

Confronting evil is one of our greatest moral responsibilities. Many of the world's most revered leaders and heros are remembered because they performed this duty well, for overcoming evil is an enduring theme in our histories and literatures. But we cannot fulfill this responsibility at all—let alone well—if we do not approach it appropriately; and the visceral responses which often underlie our reactions to unjust harms are not always correct. To resolve these matters, we need to understand the issues, the elements of evil, and the options that are available to us; and then we need to draw upon our individual and collective experiences to confront evil and other forms of immorality correctly and effectively. We will not always prevail; but if we improve our skills and continue to apply them, we ought to be able to confront evil better than we collectively seem to be doing now.

INDEX